Passionate Energies

The Gerrit and Ann Smith Family
of Peterboro, New York
Through a Century of Reform

Norman Kingsford Dann, Ph.D.

Professor Emeritus
State University of New York

COPYRIGHT © 2021 BY NORMAN K. DANN

All rights reserved. No part of this book may be reproduced, distributed, or transmitted in any form or by any means, or stored in a database of retrieval system without the prior written permission of the publisher.

First Paperback Edition: July 2021
10 9 8 7 6 5 4 3 2 1

ISBN: 978-1-7330891-1-1

Donna Dorrance Burdick is a contributing editor for this title.

Dedication

This book is dedicated to all past and present Peterboro residents whose liberal thought has led them to support and work for the achievement of liberty and justice for all.

CONTENTS

Dedication iii
Preface v

PART I

The Cultivation of Moral Reform in the Nineteenth Century

~ 1 ~ The Pre-Reform Era 9
~ 2 ~ The Reform Era 27

PART II

The Participation of the Gerrit and Ann Smith Family in Nineteenth-Century Reform Movements

~ 3 ~ The Abolition of Slavery 73
~ 4 ~ Women's Rights 117
~ 5 ~ Issues Supportive of Reform 147

Epilogue 157
The Smith Family Tree 167
The Miller Family Tree 168
Notes 169
Bibliography 177
Index 181
Acknowledgements 189
About the Author 191
Other Books by Norman K. Dann 192

Preface

Taken individually or as a whole, the Gerrit and Ann Smith family of Peterboro, New York is remarkable for the high quality of the contributions they made toward the achievement of social equality among all persons. Yet few contemporary people are aware of the Smiths' concern for the welfare of others, or the intensity of their passion for human rights issues that led to many sacrifices and accomplishments.

The Smiths would be proud of that fact because they preferred to remain anonymous, and did not seek accolades of praise for what they were doing. They performed their philanthropy within the small, isolated hamlet of Peterboro, a fact that insulated them from the critical gaze of the public.

In formerly published biographies of the Smith family, I have documented the contributions of each family member to the pursuit of human rights issues. All of them—Gerrit, Ann, Elizabeth, Greene, and Gerrit's first cousin Elizabeth Cady Stanton—lived during what is called The Reform Era of the nineteenth century, roughly 1830-1865.

This book integrates information from all of those books, and summarizes the accumulated knowledge and wisdom of thirty years of research into and writing and thinking about the Smith family and its role in the long effort for the moral reform of American society.

The scope and variety of social changes taking place during that era make it one of the most exciting times in American history for study, and the fact that the Smith family played a central and powerful role in the designs for institutional change makes them a convenient focus for understanding the entire movement. They became role models for the desired moral shifts in attitude and behavior regarding the accomplishment of social equality and equitable treatment among all persons.

All of the family members left an imprint on the social institutional fabric and life of their village, county, and nation that can still be felt today. Some current residents of the hamlet of Peterboro are descendants of former slaves freed by Gerrit and Ann, and are committed to carrying on the work for freedom and justice for all.

Locally, the Smiths in the nineteenth century inaugurated new institutions designed to pursue equity: a school for African-American youth, a home for the support of impoverished children, a church free of doctrinal rules that divide people, an underground railroad station to aid escaping former slaves, and their personal home that served as a therapeutic retreat for abused human rights advocates.

In the nineteenth century, social separation and bias were so intense and rigid that few people of one category identified with others, yet there were some enlightened ones who knew that if social tensions were to be overcome or even to subside, a revolution in the moral conscience of many people would have to occur. Those who advocated reform—leaders like William Lloyd Garrison, Susan B. Anthony, Elizabeth Cady Stanton, and Gerrit Smith—faced the entrenched power of discriminatory religious, political, and economic institutions that reinforced white male supremacy. In spite of the monumental task before them, their optimism drove them on, sparking a fire of inspiration admirable in any era, and equal to the task of persisting at all costs. Although they succeeded eventually in forcing a few legal changes in the rules of the game that govern social relationships, the score of that game remained largely the same because most people either could not or would not identify in their hearts with people not like themselves.

These were the attitudinal obstacles that members of the Smith family overcame, and in that process, infused their home with a spirit of empathy and philanthropy that actually implemented the Golden Rule to always treat others as you would wish to be treated. On a daily basis, they soaked in a marinade of concern for and dedication to others less well-off and oppressed, and gladly sacrificed their resources of time, effort, caring, and money to the benefit of people who they did not know, and might never meet.

The questions asked in this book are easy to ask and difficult to answer: How did they do it? How did they navigate through the complexity of issues and people of the turbulent reform era, and still maintain—for the most part—their own sanity, welfare, and dedication? During the decades of 1830-1860, thousands of diverse people flowed through their lives in tiny Peterboro like fallen leaves moving downstream. For brief moments, visitors saw an empathic reform environment, partook of its benefits, and moved on feeling better for the experience.

This book is not designed to impress scholars of the reform movement, but is meant to kindle fires of public interest in learning more about both the history and current relevance of the issues that dominated the social lives of people who lived during the nineteenth century reform era, and to *feel* how those issues burned in the hearts of the members of the Gerrit and Ann Smith family. As such, this book is not an end in itself, but is a catalyst to arouse interest in and passion for the actualization of natural human rights inherent in personhood, thereby enabling every person to experience equality.

I will combine in my writing both documentation and imagination, both objective and subjective "data" in the attempt to illuminate both facts and feelings about people and the times.

The process of biography entails this dual expression, for as a researcher comes to know the objective facts of a person's life, subjective feelings creep in, and may be as important as the facts. As we discover the perspectives, anxieties, and concerns of an influential person or family, we shed light on not only the issues of the day, but also on the passions, infatuations, and fears of a culture, thereby fostering at least some comprehension of the direction of the arc of history.

In order to emphasize the significance of the impact of the Smith family on the human rights fabric of American society, think of it this way: the two most important social movements for human rights in United States history are the abolition movement to end slavery, and the women's rights movement to achieve equity among the two sexes. The two most powerful leaders of those two movements are Gerrit

Smith for the abolition movement, and his first cousin Elizabeth Cady Stanton for the women's rights movement, and as we will learn later, *both* of them experimented with and learned their tactics for success in Peterboro.

PART I

The Cultivation of Moral Reform in the Nineteenth Century

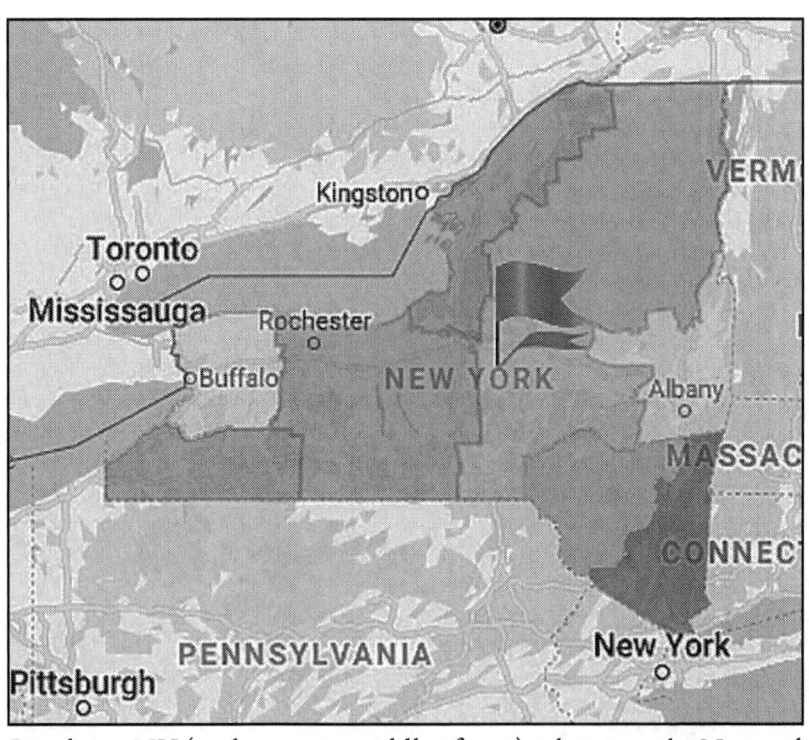

Peterboro, NY (see banner in middle of map) is home to the National Abolition Hall of Fame & Museum and the Gerrit Smith Estate. It is located close to the geographic center of New York State.

Map courtesy of discoverupstateny.com

- 1 -

The Pre-Reform Era

The story of the Gerrit and Ann Smith family and their relationship to issues of human rights starts—ironically—with one who cared very little about the rights of others, and very much about his own financial success.

Gerrit's father Peter Smith was born in Rockland County, New York in 1768. As a young man, he exhibited selfish concerns by becoming involved in the fur trade with Native Americans with his early business partner, John Jacob Astor. They both became very rich through this endeavor, eventually becoming involved together in land speculation.

Peter's attitude toward and treatment of other people was not morally attractive. He saw them as objects to be used for his own benefit, especially if they were culturally different from himself. Native Americans, poor people, black people, and non-Christians he viewed with disrespect.

An early, and more sensitive friend called him "a tenant of the wilderness" who was unaccustomed to cultural diversity, and tended to be tyrannical. He hoped that Peter would eventually learn that differences among people could be complementary in a positive way, and that "the characters of men are molded by their condition in life."

Peter had difficulty comprehending this reality, and spent much effort trying to change others to become what he preferred.[1]

A portrait of Peter Smith.
Courtesy of the Madison County Historical Society

Gerrit grew up in Peter's home observing this behavior, a fact that may have aided his development of a more tolerant and benevolent lifestyle, and may also have helped Gerrit view critically the hypocrisy that characterized the pre-reform era between the founding of the United States as an independent country and the active reform era that started around 1830.

Founding father and governor of Virginia Patrick Henry's revolutionary statement "give me liberty, or give me death," was hollow. He owned slaves. So also did our other founding heroes George Washington and Thomas Jefferson. The documents that they wrote were based on their commitment to build a government founded on the principles of equality, personal freedom, the repudiation of absolute authority, and the affirmation of an inborn, natural equality that demanded justice for all persons.

Yet the Constitution of the United States government sanctioned slavery by recognizing some people to be only 3/5 of a person. Our founders saw no contradiction in freedom for some and slavery for others. In part, this was a practical reaction to the era in which the Constitution was written, because if it had opposed slavery, it would not have been ratified. Even so, those who viewed liberty as a necessity found the state of the new nation to be intolerable.

Gerrit Smith wrote,

"How shameful the hypocrisy of our countrymen! Whilst glorying in the historical fact that our fathers were ready to take up arms against laws imposing petty taxes on tea... they nevertheless roll up the whites of their eyes in holy horror at refusals to obey laws... which sink innocent men, women and children in the hell of slavery."

Boston-based abolitionist William Lloyd Garrison publicly burned a copy of the United States Constitution in an abolition rally in Framingham, Massachusetts on July 4, 1854, thus making a loud statement about a hypocritical nation whose "parchment lies" about freedom for all needed to be debunked.[2]

Our nation, these giants of liberty declared, was founded on pretense, with a false appearance of virtue resting on claims to principles not achieved, and an intent to conceal real intentions. The new nation, founded supposedly on principles of freedom and liberty, maintained a system of oppression against black people that was perhaps unsurpassed in brutality by any other culture in world history.

We not only poured out indignities upon African-Americans, but also made it legal to do so. The growth of slavery over 300 years in the South coincided with its demise in the North, thus setting the stage for cultural conflict, and when our own laws governing the necessity of free speech, liberty, and democracy broke down in the effort to deal with those sectional differences, we killed each other in a brutal civil war as a solution.

Bias against people unlike oneself is an apathetic commitment to ignorance. It renders the mind inert, and makes liberty no more than a pretentious claim of hypocritical people. This is what the budding reformers saw, and, more importantly, *felt*, in the pre-reform revolutionary era. As poet George W. Putnam aptly put it:

"When the Briton's hand was on us,
When earth trembled at his tread,
Did our fathers crouch to wear the chain?
Go, ask the martyr'd dead!
The blood-stained plains of Lexington
Can tell the tale;—neath Bunker's sod
They sleep, whose war-cry once was, 'On!
For Freedom and for God!'
And has their proud blood in our veins
Grown still and cold?
Say, shall we stoop to wear the chains
They spurned of old?"

The more liberal thinkers of the time answered the irony of slavery and the hypocrisy of morals with action. Many parents in both the North and the South taught their children—perhaps as a function of the Second Great Awakening religious revival in the 1820s—self-criticism and the importance of the Golden Rule as the basis of a controlling conscience.

Those of this developing generation who lived in the South often left in exodus fashion for the North, thus escaping the social class domination and lack of egalitarianism that they could not stomach. This liberal-minded intelligentsia sparked the transition from a static abusive morality to a passion for the reform of corrupt social institutions.

People like James Gillespie Birney, a former slave owner turned abolitionist, moved north and supported antislavery journalism, business and politics. Angelina and Sarah Grimké, daughters of a South Carolina slave owner, moved north to become abolitionists, bold female speakers, and women's rights advocates. John Rankin moved from Tennessee to Ohio and became an educator and abolitionist, operating one of the most important underground railroad stations on the Ohio River. Such people were significant supporters of the forces that gave birth to the reform movement.

The major agents of change in the first two decades of the nineteenth century that led to the reform era of the next three decades included both philosophical and practical forces that complemented one another. The ideas inherent in perfectionism and transcendentalism fueled a popular desire for freedom of choice and expression, while the practical need to move west entailed lifestyle changes that required adjustment to new physical and social realities. In short, masses of people were ready to experiment with what they saw as new and better circumstances.

The essence of perfectionism claimed that the individual, by exercising his/her power to *select* moral behavior, could propel society toward perfect holiness and peace as if the Second Coming of Christ had already occurred. When this point was reached, coercive social institutions would no longer be needed because life would be cooperative and communal.

Such a utopian hope grew at a time near the end of the eighteenth century when societies were being convulsed with political revolutions and sweeping social change brought on by the advent of capitalism, industrialization, and systematic science. People rebelled against political and religious tyrannies of power and knowledge, and expressed new needs based in the relativity of all knowledge and the democratic establishment of rational laws based on human need and observation.

The pessimism engendered in absolute knowledge and power that had trained people to fatalistically accept poverty and control was changing into an optimism that threatened long-standing social class distinctions, and promised a better and more equitable life.

Religious and political despotisms relying on inbred authority coupled with the ignorance and superstition of the common people were challenged, and began to crumble. Formerly powerless individuals became self-empowered to make change—both personal and social—and felt that they had the responsibility to strive for societal perfection through good works, morality, benevolence, and self-sacrifice.

People began to view sin as due not to inherited depravity, but to moral depravity which they could do something about; they could choose to alter that. As they began to think about reforming themselves, they realized that if enough of them did so, society could also be reformed. And as they embraced perfectionism, they also felt the challenge of fulfilling the revolutionary promise. They had the unique opportunity to set the shape of the American cultural future by translating ideals into social reality.

Another major contributor to the impetus for reform was the philosophy of transcendentalism. Blossoming in the Boston area in the 1820s, its major tenets were belief in the inherent goodness of all people, the importance of the individual who through self-reliance can become empowered to pursue and promulgate moral goodness, and the prevalence of natural law over human-made law.

The transcendentalists like Thoreau and Emerson were concerned that existing social institutions of religion and politics corrupted people by proposing rules for behavior from contrived positions of authority. This contradicts what they felt was the natural tendency of persons to follow the Golden Rule. Such artificial institutional rules inhibit self-reliance and moral judgment, and retard the development of mutual human caring and benevolence. State and religious laws, they thought, inhibited one's natural intuitive feelings about what to do to implement the moral responsibility to bring about equitable treatment among all persons. Uninhibited freedom of action would eventually lead to the perfect social system.

The validity of such thought is certainly questionable, but its importance in this context inheres in its positive and progressive message, and in the impetus and motivation it produced for the budding reform movement.

Emerson admired Gerrit Smith for his lack of selfishness and his pursual of human equality with emphasis on natural rights—what the abolitionists referred to as a "higher law." Their notion was that any laws enacted by humans must coincide with the natural, higher law formulated supposedly by God. Therefore, laws justifying slavery were void. Both Gerrit and his cousin Elizabeth Cady Stanton respected the transcendentalists and their philosophical effort to advance reform, but worried about the lack of direct, practical effort to do so. Stanton cynically referred to "that brilliant circle of Boston transcendentalists, who hoped... to transform our selfish, competitive civilization into a Paradise where all the altruistic values might make cooperation possible."[3]

These perfectionist and transcendentalist ideas merged with and complimented the Second Great Awakening religious revival of the 1820s and early 1830s.

Prior to the 1820s, the strict authoritarianism of Puritan and Calvinist beliefs helped to prepare early settlers to endure the worst that isolated frontier life offered. Church and Sunday school attendance was required (and sometimes forced), temperance campaigns emphasized morality, and lessons contained in millions of tracts informed people of the only right way. As options diversified in the mid-1820s due to early industrialism and the advancement of science, old sources of authority weakened. Religious revivals that had been sporadic in the first two decades of the century gained in frequency and attendance, reaching a peak in the 1825-1837 period. They coincided with the new brand of Jacksonian democracy which emphasized faith that the common people could exercise political power through grassroots democratic action that could lead to justice and equality for all.

The old Federalist politics that were deferential to the elite died in the face of newfound optimism that empowered all citizens. A caste-based aristocracy was giving way to a class-based democracy that delivered the optimistic message that people working together could eventually change the oppressive conditions under which they lived.

This evangelical movement advocated persistence and hard work as antidotes to authoritative control, and avenues to individual empowerment. The process of philanthropy changed from aiding aristocratic institutions to aiding poor individuals who needed a chance to improve.

The advancement of egalitarianism brought to light some deep-seated racial and ethnic prejudices that had not previously needed overt expression in order to maintain white supremacy. Whereas options for greater social equality were expanding, so was prejudicial behavior. These coincident forces highlighted an obvious need for social reform.

Many of the people who stoked the fires of that future reform came to Central New York State as part of a mass migration from the eastern seaboard area. Between 1810 and 1840, over 6 million people migrated from east to west, bringing with them liberal religious and political ideas. As the North became more liberal-minded, the South became conservative and reactionary, thus producing a cultural contrast that made the need for reform clear.[4]

A huge stimulus to this migration came with the Treaty of Ghent. Signed in 1815, it ended the War of 1812, thereby eliminating the threat of conflict in the Central New York area. Roads and canals developed quickly thereafter, creating a psychic highway westward through the flat travel corridor between the Catskill and Adirondack mountains. In the five years following the opening of the Erie Canal between Albany and Buffalo in 1825, the population of Syracuse grew by 282%, of Buffalo by 314%, and of Rochester by 512%. As corollary developments, business and wealth increased, and feeder canals linked surrounding areas like Binghamton in the south and Oswego in the north to the Erie Canal and Central New York. Utica became a printing and publishing center with many newspapers informing thousands of families about issues and people advocating reform, and sowing seeds for it.[5]

As a settled, agrarian population developed in Central New York, people faced frequent economic insecurities, making them susceptible to revivalism that offered quick, certain answers to complex questions. The central figure feeding the revival frenzy was the preacher Charles Grandison Finney. Schooled in Connecticut and New Jersey, he apprenticed at law, took some theological study, and became a teacher. His lasting social role was that of an itinerant revival preacher. His enthusiastic sermons on salvation captured minds in need of comforting relief from anguish, and motivated people to spread the movement to others. Finney's greatest contribution to the pre-reform era—and his most meaningful legacy—was not his theology, but his techniques of mobilizing people to produce a networked social movement. Historian Whitney Cross noted that Finney "contributed more to the complexion of ensuing events" than any other force preceding the reform era.[6]

Finney worked mainly on the psychological level, converting individuals to adopt benevolent behavior. One's redemption led to concern for the mental state of other supposed sinners as people engaged in the "holy enterprise of minding other people's business." This tendency eventually morphed into benevolent organizations that took on the sociological function of humanitarianism and led to concern for the rights of whole categories of people in the 1830s. Quakers, Shakers, and various communal experiments were early signs that humanitarian motives were at least finding expression, but such groups dropped out of the larger society rather than try to reform its institutions.[7]

The religious initiative of the 1820s succeeded in developing public interest in education, with the consequence that a greater proportion of young people in Central New York attended schools than did those from other areas. This produced graduates at various levels who became writers and speakers that molded public opinion. Newspapers, magazines, journals, and religious periodicals were common, and played an important role in informing the public about social trends and recruiting them into the germinating reform movement. Around 1825, what had been scattered, local enthusiasms began to show signs of coalescence into issue areas like abolition that would attract interested people. The result, as the 1820s ended, was the transition from a pre-reform era of individually based enthusiasm, to the germination in the 1830s of a network-based array of organizations building political power to conduct great social missions in the ensuing reform era.[8]

The 1830s dawned having been primed for serious reform activity by at least two decades of work by a bevy of moral preachers that focused on individual sin. Their evangelism got its start in the Presbyterian tradition, but spread quickly to all denominations. Preachers like Finney, Jedediah Burchard, James Boyle, and Orestes Brownson bathed the Central New York area with anxiety about morality. And to their advantage, the prevailing cultural attitude engendered optimism—the belief that change is possible and that one's condition in life can get better.

Democratic ideals and practices in this Jacksonian era were exploding onto the social scene with glowing imperatives for experimentation with new values and lifestyles. People wanted to know—could the abolition of slavery work for our benefit? Could women really be equal to men in intelligence and ability? Could temperance improve the moral quality of life?

And they even seemed willing to put these questions to the test through seriously organized social work. This symbolized a major shift in perspective from the religion-based evangelistic belief that individual sin produces an immoral society, to the reformer's belief that an immoral society produces individual sin. In sum, religion was still important in shaping morality, but the dominant perspective was shifting from its psychological benefits for an individual, to its sociological benefits for society. The misplaced evangelistic fervor over individual sin entailed its own defeat because a group-based and networked social movement was a necessary precedent for the societal change that they desired.

The gigantic irony in this misplaced fervor is as follows: Both evangelistic religion and conservative politics are individualistically oriented. That is, they focus on psychological benefits or profits for individual persons. The excessive individualism of the adherents of evangelistic religion tricks them into support of conservative politics. This deception prevents the social achievement of their goals of morality when the conservative party wins because its policy focus is on competitive success and profit for individuals, instead of the welfare of the whole social body. Interestingly, this same fault today makes allies of evangelistic religion and Republican Party politics, which negates the collectively-based moral changes that they advocate.

Forces at work in the 1830s caused many people to shift their focus from personal needs to those of society. When churches refused to support the abolition of slavery, members dropped out but took their passion for moral change with them. Their previously misguided, individually focused zeal coalesced into reform power. Whereas individually expressed zeal in a religious setting was accepted as a sign of passion, socially expressed zeal by reformers was frowned upon as a sign of mental imbalance. Religious fervor was OK, but social fervor was not because if the reformers were successful, the move toward social equality would threaten the position and status of some individuals.

Reformers were aware of the source of their opposition, and did not mind being labeled as mad or crazy. They knew that their long-term goals were worth the effort, and viewed being regarded as eccentric as a badge of honor. Criticism of their work only reinforced its value. It never deterred them. As the 1840s approached, they found increasing support. Their idealistic desire for a better, more moral society was deeply ingrained in the early nineteenth century American mind, so when the technique of evangelism failed, people felt not defeated, but motivated to try something else. The Second Great Awakening era of the 1820s and 1830s had polarized the sacred/profane positions, thus guiding the issues and people toward the political arena.

The issues prevalent in the early 1840s caused people to think less about supernatural things and more about practical needs in the present. Severe economic depression, war in the southwest, and the extension of slavery—or even its abolition—were important political issues. Attitudes shifted away from the conservative Democratic Party and toward the more liberal Whig positions. People showed a growing interest in national and international affairs, with a consequently diminished interest in life in the next world. As sure signs of this shift, tactics for temperance turned from moral suasion to legal compulsion, and most abolitionists abandoned moral suasion for political activity. The Union or Free Church movement epitomized the tactical transition from psychological to sociological tactics necessary to implement reform. While it held on to Christian principles, its orientation was practical regarding social change. The label "Free" referred to its freedom from sectarian doctrine, a force that separated people rather than uniting them. This move stimulated the process of coalition. The Free Church also melded religion and politics, and became a forum for abolitionism. As such, it acted as a structured antislavery organization, fully supporting the new antislavery Liberty Party. This church was a base for networking among abolitionists, and drew former evangelicals into its fold. It emphasized the notion that whereas conversion of an individual was exciting, reform of a society was humanitarian.

In summary for the pre-reform era, the perfectionists, the transcendentalists, and the Second Great Awakening ignited a quality of activism in religion that sent people searching for areas of application for their ideas of morality. They eventually were drawn toward the more practical human rights movements advocating abolition and women's rights. They found similarity between their philosophical ideas and the reformers' political ideas, and the merger was a necessary step in the process of building a successful social movement. They all believed in these forces: the value of the individual as an informed, democratic citizen; optimism regarding the possibility of change; the process of devaluing self-centeredness, authoritative hierarchies, and fatalism; individual empowerment and the equality of all persons, and they worked diligently to unite many factions into a coherent effort to make possible the pursuit of life, liberty, and happiness.

All of these previously covered forces were at work in the early decades of the nineteenth century to mold the minds of people, especially young people like Gerrit Smith and Ann Carroll Fitzhugh. Born

"The Hive," birthplace of Ann Carroll Fitzhugh in Chewsville, Maryland.
Photo courtesy of the Maryland Historical Trust

---

in 1797 and 1805 respectively, they both grew up amid a whirlwind of competing ideas.[9]

Ann was reared in the slave state of Maryland by the wealthy William Frisby Fitzhugh family, owners of over sixty slaves. As a young person, she witnessed the horrors of slavery firsthand. When Ann was twelve in 1817, the Fitzhugh family sold their Maryland property and most of their slaves and moved to the western New York frontier area near what would become the city of Rochester. William Fitzhugh and two of his Hagerstown, Maryland business associates, Charles Carroll and Nathaniel Rochester, founded the city of Rochester at the "100 acre tract" which they had purchased in 1803.

After the move to the emerging Rochester area, young Ann saw through personal experience the full contrast between slave life and free life, and committed herself in a supportive role to any plan to advance freedom for all. She was also deeply influenced by the religious movements of that time, and became committed to Christianity.

A photo of Ann Carroll Fitzhugh Smith.
From the author's collection

Ann's connection with the youthful Gerrit Smith occurred through Gerrit's first wife, Wealtha Backus. Wealtha's brother, Frederick, had married Ann's sister, Rebecca. When Gerrit and Wealtha married in 1819, Gerrit met Rebecca and her 13-year-old sister, Ann. Three years after Wealtha's early death in late 1819, Gerrit and Ann married.

Ann's early religious training clashed with Gerrit's highly secular young life. In the mid-1820s, she guided him into adopting the Christian faith. That system of beliefs remained with him in varying degrees throughout his life. Whereas Ann found solace in religion continually, Gerrit became more skeptical of it as he aged.

Their only child born during this pre-reform era that lived through adulthood was Elizabeth Smith, born September 20, 1822. The revival fervor had little effect on her young mind, and throughout her life she, like her father, was guardedly skeptical of the value of religion, although she supported and worked for the two major human rights movements of her later life—abolition and women's rights.[10]

The long-term effect of the major forces of the pre-reform era was to prepare human minds for impending convulsive social changes. Perfectionist ideas, new philosophies, and enthusiastic religious revivals had pressured people to think differently, and provided momentum for bold steps into uncharted social territory. Old habits and authority structures melted under the heat of new emphasis on liberty and equality as social life moved into the reform era.

- 2 -

The Reform Era

The 1830s dawned on a new day—an exciting time of rising expectations for everyone, but especially for people outside of the elite class. With new leaders placing emphasis on the moral necessity of equitable treatment of all persons, even those most intensely discriminated against could sense hope. As players in a moral drama anchored in reality, those less well-off began to have new feelings. Despair was diminished by aspiration, defeat seemed less certain, and despondency became mitigated by anticipation. Perhaps, they thought, the future actually could resemble something closer to the Golden Rule.

The new style of thought was not like the old, muted opposition to the philosophical sin of religions, but a loud shout against physical and social abuse carried out with malice. Humane ideas about the welfare of all persons trumped the old emphasis on personal gain and profit. For those who identified with the spirit of reform, the old male habit of being defined in macho terms of patriarchy, honor, and prideful public display, gave way to a somewhat feminizing trend that emphasized such honorable traits as benevolence, empathy, and compassion.

These new reform era players, especially the leaders, were iconoclastic moral critics who stood outside of "the establishment," unworried and unencumbered with concerns for their own success as politicians or businessmen. Their object was to proclaim the truth as they saw it. They were agitators exposing social corruption and inertia in a new era which was bent on experimenting with ideas and social plans.

As time passed, reformers moved back and forth across what appeared to some to be boundaries between idealism and real life. Utopias mixed with practicality; dreams sweetened the fabric of discriminatory reality; thinkers became actors as they tried to implement their visions of justice and equality; communes blossomed to supposedly make social life perfect; common people became uncommonly dedicated to causes to help people they would never know, and committed their resources to programs of social change that could revolutionize life.

In this boiling mix of ideas and action, contradictions abounded. Antislavery activists worshiped in pro-slavery churches; egalitarian politicians worked within discriminatory parties; the traditionally second class, quiet female citizen made public antislavery and pro-suffrage speeches, and wore bloomers to challenge male dominance.

Such experiments with new and shocking ideas made reformers' thoughts and actions look inconsistent. It is no wonder that they were seen as incompetent or fanatical. There were no historical precedents for reform movements, so they were often conflicted and unsure of how to do what they were certain needed to be done. Their democratic and sometimes socialist ideas intertwined in a confusing web of new and developing institutions that sought new and better circumstances for the oppressed. Their dreams for the abolition of slavery, equal rights for women, and the accomplishment of temperance became not just moral slogans, but scripts for action amid unbridled optimism.

Optimism and action were attractive traits to masses of people who wanted change, and the message of the reformers was being spread widely by a variety of circumstances in the 1830s. A severe and prolonged economic depression stimulated millions of people to see the need for change, and extensive developments in communicative options both informed people about potential reforms, and recruited them to support the movement.

Newspapers multiplied rapidly in the 1830-1840 period, especially in response to increasing interest in reform issues. Because newspapers were one of the few sources of news in the nineteenth century, they were powerful organs of public opinion formation. Periodicals of reform organizations helped spread information among those who could afford them. Improvements in roads, and expansion of railroads connected formerly isolated locations. Public speakers on reform issues became an important source of news and entertainment as they traveled throughout the country. In fact, reform leaders like Frederick Douglass, Gerrit Smith, or Elizabeth Cady Stanton had the status of current rock stars when they appeared in various cities. They attracted crowds of thousands in outdoor settings to share the latest ideas for abolition or temperance. Canals carried people and ideas, and hundreds of new organizations at local levels mobilized people to participate in a growing array of reform causes.

All of these avenues of information networked into a communicative web that recruited thousands into the reform cause, and channeled their anguish, zeal, and hope into potential change for the future.

As they moved westward, former New Englanders faced cultural shock. Their former institutional habits could not cope with frontier conditions, and as they found help and guidance in the reform movement, they asked themselves new questions that lubricated their insertion into reform activity. Is slavery okay? Are women citizens? Are poor people equals?

These questions began to make sense in the 1830s as reform efforts took shape, and even made change seem plausible. Elizabeth Cady Stanton noted that she was grateful to live at a time when reform was possible. She and her cousin Gerrit Smith devised a pattern by which reform might actually have widespread affect: 1—reform oneself; 2—reform one's family; 3—reform one's community; 4—reform the nation. The obvious theme was to pursue moral reform and social change by setting local examples that other individuals, families, or communities could emulate. This was actually a gentle form of persuasion. Both Cady Stanton and Smith valued self-sovereignty, wanting others to choose the better moral path once they had seen it.

Although they held radical ideas, most reformers were cautious in rejecting the status quo, and proposed suggestions that others could adopt. Leaders like Smith believed in establishing new institutions at the local level that would act as beacons to guide others in the direction of moral change. In Peterboro, he established a school for young black people, a group home to support economically destitute children, a church free of sectarian division, a temperance hotel to reduce the problem of drunkenness, and an underground railroad station to aid escaping former slaves. And importantly, he did all this with the total support of his wife and children.

Both Cady Stanton and Smith were good personifications of the model reformer. They saw hypocrisy and tried to remedy it. They saw discrimination and tried to mollify it. They saw injustice and tried to reverse it. They saw hate and tried to soften it. As agitators, they created public awareness of inequality and mistreatment, and helped formulate policies that politicians might implement. They tried to meld the agitator's quest for the desirable with the politician's art of the possible—a process so difficult to achieve that it becomes clear why some groups simply dropped out of the existing institutional structure to accomplish such goals in communes.

Reformers did succeed in introducing a vitality to democracy by flavoring their utopian vision with an optimistic faith in the general public to choose the more moral pathway. The risks they took to their resources and reputation were clearly understood, but their appeal to practical reason made them feel that they would eventually prevail. One critical factor in the reform game that they did not perceive clearly was the intensity of the entrenched prejudice that they were fighting against. Regarding abolition, for instance, the naïvely optimistic reform leaders believed originally that moral suasion could convince slave owners of the sin of owning people, and they would repent. Slave owners actually regarded slave ownership as a source of prestige and respect, as well as lucrative profit. Their perception of black people was so low that they viewed slavery as an easy solution to both the labor and the race problem. The reformers' belief that slave owners had innate moral tendencies that would lead them toward voluntary emancipation was in error.

Most of the reformers as adults had developed a sense of personal and economic security in stable communities, and were accustomed to seeing their influence produce results. Gerrit preferred to see quick, tangible results of his philanthropy, so when social change was slow to occur, he felt frustrated. But much to the credit of reformers, their most valuable virtue was persistence. In the face of social, political, economic, and sometimes physical defeat, they just brushed off the insults, healed various types of wounds, and plodded on. They worked constantly to keep the issues alive and in the face of the public. Although their progressive, liberal ideas bothered conservatives and got them labeled as lunatics, they did not mind. These leaders were men and women who were usually well-educated, fairly prosperous, and worked at respectable jobs as professionals, skilled laborers, and proprietors. They dedicated their security, their personal well-being, and their resources—some of which were fortunes—to notions of progressive morality to improve the lives of thousands not like themselves.

The reformers were not good at prophecy, but became expert at influencing the moral thought of others. With unswerving confidence in their rightness, and a relentless faith in the power of ideas to win over the selfishness of discrimination and profit, they strove toward the transformation of the fundamental political, religious, and economic institutions of a whole society.

In Gerrit Smith's case, some of his fellow reformers criticized him for using money—his major resource—to help bring about reform goals. That pained him, but did not stop him from combining that brand of philanthropy with his intense empathy for oppressed people. One reform colleague and close friend of Gerrit was Peterboro resident and abolitionist James Caleb Jackson. He wrote,

"To no man of the Nineteenth century... does the democratic idea, 'that to be a man proves that one has all the rights of a man,' owe so much for its defense and its advancement as to Mr. Smith. He dug it out of its grave... and it came back... to cheer the fainthearted, encourage the desponding, strengthen the weak, and become once more the rallying cry—the symbol of might and majesty among men."

And in like fashion, as a kudos to all reformers, Harriet Jacobs, a young slave woman who had hidden due to fear of the sexual advances of her owner, wrote,

> "There are noble men and women who plead for us, striving to help those who cannot help themselves. God bless them! God give them strength and courage to go on!"[1]

And go on they did! The themes that attracted their attention, and the choices that motivated their passion-driven action were many, and varied over time. This sometimes confuses readers and researchers. We must keep in mind that the scope of morally based changes that they advocated was wide-reaching, and a given reformer—perhaps Gerrit Smith—might hop around among various issues depending on the relevant social circumstances. An abolition rally, for instance, might also entail opportunities to moralize about Free Church religion and politics, or temperance, or women's rights. All of these topics were interrelated, and to speak about one engendered speaking about all of them.

Indeed, other themes also motivated reform work. Diet change was advocated as being important to physical and mental health; dress reform for women was a possible route to more feminine social and political power; water cure and movement cure facilities might aid one's personal health; freedom from tobacco use often accompanied lectures on temperance; boycotting the products of slave labor might affect the economics of slavery; spiritualists, Millerites, and Shakers advocated their own peculiar paths to a better life.

In addition to these specific changes desired, there were also overarching themes that characterized all aspects of the reform era. Probably its most important theme was the emphasis on the reality of natural, inborn human rights based in the fact of one's personhood. In their writings, reformers often capitalized the word Natural to draw attention to its significance. The combination of evangelical religion, the passion of reformers, and the idea of natural rights produced a powerful intellectual/moral force. A classic statement from Gerrit

Smith illustrated its motivational power: "To no human charter am I indebted for my rights." Governments, he claimed, could neither grant nor restrict natural rights. They could only protect them.

Other master themes of reform included the freedom of the individual as a sovereign, self-actualizing person as the foundation of democratic institutions. Such an idea contradicted past traditions of powerful rulers, and reinforced the intentions of our governmental founders. This liberal theme challenged rigid caste relationships, such as those existing amid slavery, and proposed the pursuit of equality among all persons as the goal.

These themes infused the reform era with hope, a necessity for recruiting underprivileged people into the movement. Players in the movement expressed a brand of radicalism and action that fueled their expectation of success. With an arrogant sense of confidence, they fought against colossal and entrenched discriminatory institutions, convinced that they would eventually translate their passion into political expression that could change old and long-accepted cultural habits. Realizing that all of the proposed reforms were interdependent, they forged ahead knowing that regardless of the topic, they were all striving for the same goal: a moral society in which mutual caring is always the basis of action.

The goal of this book is to relate the Gerrit and Ann Smith family to this complex reform era in a way that highlights their significance in the decades-long drama. Whereas many families of that time harbored members who were recognized as reformers, the uniqueness of the Smith family rests in the fact that they all became known nationally for their participation in some aspect of social reform.

Gerrit, Ann, and Elizabeth worked mainly in the human rights areas of abolition and women's rights. Greene spent his short life working in scientifically-based endeavors to inform the public on the importance of species diversity in the natural world, and to protect and preserve both the flora and fauna of ecosystems. Peter Smith, Sr. predated the reform era, but the work he did to build a lucrative land

Gerrit Smith at the age of 48 (left) in 1845, and in his 70s.
Photos from the author's collection

sale business set the foundation that allowed his succeeding generations to have a resource base that would permit them to become influential in their chosen fields.

A main identifying trait of the Smith family was its deep empathy for all persons—but especially for those who were in any way oppressed. They followed Gerrit's lead in applying what he called the "self-application rule." That is, observe what is happening to people around you, and apply it to oneself to see how it feels. Would you approve? If not, do something about it for that other person. He was fond of saying that the Golden Rule is the only one we need to guide moral behavior.

The Smiths cultivated friendships and alliances with those who opposed them, always recognizing their best qualities, and refused to hold grudges against anyone. For these leaders of reform, the true test of their commitment to a cause was not going to be the judgment of future generations, but the degree to which their own lives reflected the values and changes that they espoused. One's private life became a practical application of moral dreams of a better society, which they sincerely believed was achievable at home. Their personal life operated on principles of acceptance, tolerance, and empathy instead of patriarchy, power, and privilege. They created in their home what those who formed communes hoped to accomplish by dropping out of society. The Smiths' wealth enabled aristocratic potential, but they were humble in both habits and consumption. As the larger culture's concerns for individual power and success developed, they focused on using their resources to foster equality. In essence, they challenged the status quo with love for everyone, and loathing of discrimination. A visitor to the Smith home in 1870 remarked:

"I have visited many houses... but never before one like this. One breathing the affluence of wealth without a touch of its insolence, characterized by refinement and the highest culture, yet free from all the impertinence of display. Plainness of attire, simplicity of manner, absolute sincerity, and an all-pervading spirit of love characterize the family and give tone to the home—a home free from press and hurry and confusion, where differences of opinion are expressed without irritation, where the individual is respected, where the younger members of the family are reverent and the older ones considerate, where all are mindful of the interests of each, and each is thoughtful for all."[2]

Their internal family dynamics exhibited marvels of communication. They had daily talk sessions with one another at the dining table, and in the parlor at evening time. Their talk not only stimulated and soothed one another, but in a non-electronic era, was also entertaining, and the thoughts and ideas shared were educational. They did have the notion that they were community moral leaders guiding a local—and hopefully wider—flock toward more caring ways of thinking and acting.

When apart, family members wrote letters to one another daily—thousands of which survive in the collection of family papers.[3] Letters were serial accounts of a day's activities and thoughts—a form of "talking" with the other person as if s/he were present. Such letters were cathartic for the writer, and therapeutic for the reader. They were full of feelings as well as words, and served to maintain loving contact with each other. Letters were expected and looked forward to with high anticipation, and when they did not arrive, family members would chastise one another for not exercising that caring motif.

They also wrote to one another in poetic fashion. All family members delighted in writing to one another what they called "rhymes." It usually occurred on special occasions such as birthdays, anniversaries, or holidays, but could occur at any time. The rhymes were usually loving recognitions of the value of relationships between them, but sometimes contained deep personal concerns.

Ann's birthday poem to Gerrit in 1848 read:
"Think not the day can pass unheeded,
Best loved of all below,
The frosts of time have not impeded
My warm love in its flow.

O no! While frosts of time are flinging
O'er weak love chills + blight—
To mine they are forever bringing
Sweetness + new delight."

And as another example, Gerrit's poem to Ann on their thirty-seventh anniversary in 1859:
"The years are thirty-seven, my Fraw,
Since Parson Cummings clasped our hands;
And I did gladly thee endow
With all my cash, + stocks, + lands.

But though so many they have been,
Each year has prov'd a precious boon
Our married life the world has seen
To be a lifelong honeymoon."

There are hundreds of these poems collected in a "Verse Book" in the Gerrit Smith papers. They reveal the full spectrum of emotions among family members. When Ann and Gerrit had a mid-life crisis in the relationship, Gerrit lamented:
"This day makes two and thirty years
Since I this wonderous woman wed.
'Tis proved by my briney tears
I'de better kept my single bed."

Ann responded:
"A nation now doth sing thy praise
Still thou wilt not forget the lays
Wherewith in quiet humbler days
I sought to make thee glad.

And wilt thou welcome once again
My offering poor, in which I'de fain
Express my love, but all in vain—
The future makes me sad."

Gerrit wrote the introduction to the Verse Book: "These rhymes will be prized by our successors because they will reveal one of the ways in which the members of our family sought to interest + gratify each other, + thus one of the ways of enabling them to form opinions of the tastes, habits, + character of our family."

The reason that he called them "rhymes" instead of poetry was because he was certain that they carried little literary quality. As he put it:
"I crawl on [earth's] surface + lie in its dust
Asham'd that my soul will not soar.
I try to write Stanzas—but oh they are just
Most wretched of rhymes—nothing more."

One important certainty about the Smith family is that they stayed in touch with one another emotionally, even when they were apart physically. They talked often about personal issues, and also about the social reform issues of the day. At evening time they would gather together in the parlor, or on the front porch, or in the winter, around the warmth of a fireplace, and discuss heavy social and political issues. And when important visitors like Charles Sumner, John Brown, or Elizabeth Cady Stanton were present, the discussions revolved around reform topics that would eventually reweave the social fabric of life in the United States.

The Smith "family" even included the hired help. Housekeepers and child attendants lived in the mansion with the Smiths—especially during the winter—and were called "Aunt Betsey," or "Aunt Lolly." As adults, Elizabeth and Greene Smith recalled intimate moments and important learning experiences with these extended family members. And the entire clan was a happy group, exhibiting no feelings of inferiority, low anxiety, a healthy sense of gratitude for the connections with each other, humane benevolence toward each other, and a high spirit of optimism and humility.

These paid servant members of the household adopted the reform goals of the Smiths. This is an important point regarding mutual support in their complex reform efforts against the sometimes-overwhelming tendency to discriminate coming from the outside culture. The Smith family was often considered to be a bunch of idiosyncratic fools who wasted huge amounts of time, effort, and money. It was their commitment to reform activity that helped to assure them that they were all part of a congregation with an historic mission for which their in-group was therapeutic. They knew that they were taking risks by committing themselves to helping oppressed persons, but the dignity and respect that flowed among all family members underpinned their actions and their love for one another. And when other players in the reform effort needed support, they often visited or wrote to the Smiths to receive their soothing reassurance.

The two main players and leaders in the family were, of course, Gerrit and Ann.

Gerrit was born in Utica to Peter and Elizabeth Livingston Smith on March 6, 1797, just two days after George Washington left the office of President of the United States. As a member of the generation that succeeded our revolutionary founders, Gerrit would, as a young man, be faced with the possibility of becoming an active player in the reform era.

When he purchased his father's land sale business just after his graduation from Hamilton College in 1818, he became the manager of a large and relatively steady income. At this early age he was concerned about the plight of people who were oppressed, and decided to dedicate a large portion of his financial resource to improving their life circumstances. Why he was benevolent and philanthropic is still a matter of conjecture, but recent research has shed some light on possible causes.

Much of what we have assumed in the past to be learned behavior is now being challenged by new discoveries in the field of genetics. It is clear that persons do inherit tendencies toward developing certain patterns of behavior. Alcoholism, for instance, is known to be an inherited tendency, although it may not develop if the social circumstances to stimulate it are not present. The masculine/feminine traits of gender that characterize one's preferred lifestyle are inherited, as is one's preferred choice of a sexual partner.

It seems likely that there is a genetic factor at work in determining whether one is a caring or a selfish person. Research has been done that connects one's degree of empathy and caring for others to the neural complexity of the amygdala in the human brain. My attempts to account for Gerrit's philanthropy by reference to social factors are weak. His father Peter exhibited no philanthropy, was avaricious, and used others for his own benefit. His mother Elizabeth did show caring toward others, but was a minor influence on Gerrit because of Peter's intent to groom him as a future businessman, and also because she died in 1818 just as Gerrit was making major life choices. She may, however, have been the source of Gerrit's caring gene. Gerrit Smith's first biographer was a family friend who knew him well, and in 1878 Octavius Brooks Frothingham give us a hint as to what he believed to be the cause of Gerrit's philanthropy: "Nature made him a philanthropist." His reference to "nature" infers natural cause, and reinforces the role of genetics.

Whatever the explanation of his philanthropy might be, Gerrit became recognized internationally as one of the most important leaders of the moral reform era in the United States. He often received front page attention in city newspapers throughout the country, and even abroad.

In the issue area of human rights, he produced significant writings and oratory, and combined those achievements with such high intensity of emotional passion that the public was kept well aware of reform trends. Gerrit was respected throughout reform circles of acquaintances, as well as by the less educated general public. The power he wielded through the use of his money in philanthropic ways made him one of the most powerful—if not *the* most powerful—reformer of the era.

In spite of Gerrit Smith's enormous social power and influence during the reform era, his accomplishments and legacy were lost to all but the most diligent nineteenth century professional historians. How could that happen? The answer is: that is the way he wanted it. He intentionally stayed in tiny, isolated Peterboro rather than travel to regional or national meetings, conferences, and conventions. He did not want to be recognized by the public for his acts of charity, and intentionally stayed out of public life. He refused to seek political office, even though many people in high political office begged him to do so.

Smith also chose carefully the targets for his philanthropy. He declined to give money to large institutions that might carry his name. Ezra Cornell sought Gerrit's financial aid in building Cornell University, but Gerrit refused in part because he was certain they would name something after him. He preferred to give away his money in small amounts, to relatively insignificant people. That way, his actions would not make much news, and he could see tangible results of his philanthropy quickly. He helped the oppressed—poor people, sick people, runaway slaves, and women—and expected nothing in return. During his lifetime, he gave away approximately one billion dollars as measured against our dollars today. And yet, history books barely mention him—and he would be very pleased to know that.

Smith saw early America as "The home of the free and the land of the oppressed." He might have sung, "My country 'tis of thee, sweet land of bigotry." He believed that attitudes toward women and black people were so toxic that every citizen's mental state was poisoned with prejudice. He knew that he was in a small minority of people who opposed those prejudices, but he could not resist the battle. Failure neither changed his mind, nor taught him to quit. And finally, today, we research and write his life's story to show his significance to his own generation, and to emphasize the relevance of his ideas and actions to our current dilemmas. One of his contemporary abolitionist colleagues, Lewis Tappan, wrote to him in 1842,

"I have often thought that you and your dear family have made many sacrifices, [and] I know it gratified you to act on the principle—it is more blessed to give than to receive."[4]

Gerrit's approach to reform work was guided by his belief that any doctrine or dogma led one to accept biases that hurt other people. Therefore, he opposed political or denominational loyalties as pernicious in their effect. He established the nondenominational Free Church of Peterboro to attract generic Christians instead of Baptists, Methodists, or Presbyterians, and although he was the major founder of the political Liberty Party, he never agreed to be considered a member of it or of any other party. He felt that the

"responsibilities of [allegiance to] party [or denomination] take the place of the definite and deeply conscious responsibilities of the individual. When our countrymen shall have risen to this higher plane of character there will be Christians instead of [denominational adherents], and patriots instead of Republicans [and] Democrats...."[5]

The Free Church of Peterboro was Gerrit Smith's attempt to place Christianity over loyalty to denomnation. He made a simlar stand against political parties.

From the author's collection

A major feature of this non-discriminatory type of thought was Gerrit's ability to integrate culturally accepted dichotomies—an admirable accomplishment for his time, or for *any* time. This feat required a huge amount of empathy. He crossed social boundaries that most people saw as important to maintaining their own status. He broke down the overbearing pattern of dualistic thinking that separates people, and thereby had the perceptive ability to unify black and white, masculine and feminine, sacred and profane, utopian and realistic, natural and social worlds.

As examples, Smith talked about *persons* instead of blacks and whites; he noted that women could be masculine and men could be feminine; he created a church that united religion and politics; he opted for a utopian state of morality in society through such practical means as intersex and interracial education; he saw balance among diverse elements in the natural world, and transferred the idea to seeing balance among diverse people in the social world.

He was able to perceive, and tried to implement, the fundamental integration and interdependence of all social and physical elements in his vision of a combined natural/social system. This yin-yang view of reality expressed his unquenchable optimism about and faith in each individual to opt for social justice and equality. He felt certain that the moral being within each individual would carry the day in a formula that seemed to him to make reform oriented social change possible. It was because of this idealistic vision that his critics called him mad or crazy.

This vision of the possibility of a more perfect social world drove him on in the face of frustration with what he saw as public apathy for the causes of oppressed people. As he projected his own ideas on to others, he refused to believe that they could not be inspired into perceiving the negative effects of their own biases, and once that happened, reform would be inevitable. He thought that the moral example that he and his family set would be adequate to convince others to do likewise. Most likely, his isolated social position in Peterboro insulated him against the fact that many citizens were like his father—self-centered, biased, and comfortable.

Nevertheless, Gerrit plodded on in his lifelong dedication to reform via use of the one hugely influential tool that he had—money. With it, he lubricated the wheels of change hoping for the best, and when he failed, he was not disillusioned, but was only motivated to try harder. He used money as a resource that belonged to others, seeing it not as his, but as a divine gift to be used for the common good. When criticized about his continual attempt to change things, he claimed that rather than just accepting social conditions as they are, we should labor to leave them better than we found them. One observer called him "a steady geyser of reform." Indeed, he could not keep himself from erupting.

One of the more interesting aspects of Gerrit's reform model was his idea of equating the natural world with the social world. He saw both balance and change as constant aspects of nature. Balance exists among diverse elements of a natural system, yet it is always in flux. Nothing is static, and change is constant. What exists at any moment is not necessarily right or permanent, and the continuing balance among all of a natural system's elements depends upon its diversity. This analogy, he thought, could be a model for guiding our thought about society. The diverse social elements are race, ethnicity, social class, age, sex, gender, and the like. Rather than use these elements as reasons to separate people, perhaps we could see them as complimenting one another so that no one of them can dominate. If that attitude could develop, then reform of biased institutions would be possible.

Another important feature of Gerrit's style of reform activity was his willingness to admit failure and switch tactics. His critics called him indecisive and weak because he vacillated among various techniques of action. Actually, it was more a sign of strength than weakness. For instance, in his pursuit of the abolition of slavery, when it became clear that moral suasion was not working, he switched to the use of political tactics. Such flexibility allowed adjustment to changing conditions rather than stumbling along using outmoded tactics.

Gerrit's skill with the use of words was a major advantage in this age of oratory. As a boy, he was coached in the art of public speaking by his father. Peter was a successful stage actor in New York City as a young man, and knew the value of powerful public speaking. In 1854, a newspaper reporter with the <u>Philadelphia Register</u> commented:

> "I never beheld Gerrit Smith until the assembling of the present Congress, and I was then prepared from what I had heard, to look upon an ascetic dogmatist and arbitrary man of cranks... and eccentricities. Never did I realize a more complete or more gratifying disappointment. I found in him a man whose identity I would not exchange for that of any other man upon whom my eyes have ever looked.... I have never seen a man whose presence [shows] impressive dignity,... intelligence and genius, without the seeming consciousness of either; [he exhibits] benevolence and courtesy upon which no shadow ever seems to fall, and a courage so constant and unfailing that it never needs the fuel of intolerance or anger to sustain it.... When he speaks none are inattentive to him. No man can doubt the sincerity of his look, [or ignore] the deep, rich and thrilling tones of his voice. No

man for a moment can fail to appreciate the thoughts he utters, in language all simplicity and dignity. Many smile at and some deride the 'ultraism' of the sentiments he utters, but these very men are among the foremost to acknowledge the greatness of his intellectual and moral nature."[6]

A Peterboro friend who became Gerrit's first biographer said of him, "Not to have visited Gerrit Smith at home, not to have received his hearty greeting at the door, not to have seen him glowing and beaming at his porch, not to have heard his copious table-talk is to have missed one of the satisfactions of life."[7]

People who watched the example of social perfection (as he would put it) that he exhibited through his lifestyle felt revitalized and drawn toward the process of moral reform themselves. It is no wonder that when Gerrit proposed marriage to 16-year-old Ann Carroll Fitzhugh—eight years younger than he—Ann's father William F. Fitzhugh was delighted. He wrote to Peter Smith,

"Entertaining no doubt that your son Mr. Gerrit Smith has made you acquainted with his intention of [making] a connection with my family by marriage with my daughter Ann, and that such a measure meets your approbation—I deem it respectful to assure you of the high consideration with which we regard him and that it is with our consent and best wishes he is so shortly to become one of us."[8]

Ann became, at the early date of January 3, 1822, a significant player in the life of Gerrit Smith, and in the reform movement that would shape New York State history for the next four and a half decades.

Ann was born on January 11, 1805 in the Maryland slave-holding family of William Frisby Fitzhugh and Anne Hughes Fitzhugh. She was the ninth of twelve children reared by the ambitious and entrepreneurial Fitzhugh family. As the nineteenth century dawned, William F. Fitzhugh and two of his slave-holding Hagerstown friends were making plans to get out of the slave-holding business.

In 1803, William F. Fitzhugh, Charles Carroll, and Nathaniel Rochester purchased one hundred acres of land on the Genesee River in Upstate New York. Because of water power availability, the location was ripe for business development.

After the War of 1812 ended in 1815, the three men sold their Maryland land and their slaves and moved to the new settlement of Rochester. Fitzhugh moved his family there in 1817 when Ann was twelve years old. Importantly, she had grown up as a child in slave culture, thereby obtaining a clear picture of the horrors of slavery.

As the wife of a powerful male reformer, Ann filled the role of his "support staff." She managed the domestic affairs of their house as a "First Lady" in charge of hired servants, social manners, physical decor, and reception of guests. Her rearing in a male-dominated plantation family had prepared her for subservient status. For most of her life, she accepted her status as being legitimately quiet, delicate, subordinate, domestic, religious, maternal, and—maybe most importantly—idle.

These roles were common for women in aristocratic families, and led to an unfortunate set of circumstances for future historians attempting to conduct research into their lives. At the time of Ann's life, women were considered to be insignificant in institutional life outside of the family. Their identity grew out of the males with whom they were associated. When a woman married, she lost her name, her right to own property, and her voice in public gatherings. Ann Carroll Fitzhugh became Mrs. Gerrit Smith, and derived her status and reputation through him. She needed his permission to travel, spend money, become involved in public activity, and, of course, could not vote.

One result of this discrimination against women is the lack of written records of what they said or did. For the Smith family, libraries and historical societies have collections of Gerrit Smith Papers, Greene Smith Papers, and Peter Smith Papers, but no collections of papers for Ann or Elizabeth. To learn about the lives of the women, one must dig through hundreds of boxes of papers assigned to the males in order to ferret out

Gerrit and Ann Smith, in a carte de visite, from the 1870s. Cartes de visite were small albumen prints that were mounted on 2 1/2 x 4-inch cards. They replaced ambrotypes and Daguerreotypes as an easy means of sending photographs through the mail and exchanging them with friends to be posted in their photo albums.

From the author's collection

tidbits of information relevant to the females. There are very few newspaper articles with references to women; such articles are a major source of information regarding the doings and accomplishments of males.

The result of such demeaning treatment of women was a sense of worthlessness and ineffectiveness for anything outside of their assigned domestic duties. Ann sometimes signed off on her letters to Gerrit as "Your useless wife." And this was in the face of the fact that Gerrit considered her to be physically attractive and an equal person to himself. At least that is what he wrote and said in public.

However, he was often critical of her ways and ideas, and called her his "Pale Flower," or "my dear angel wife." In her letters to Gerrit, she frequently signed off as "Your attached wife," a signal that she felt leashed and accountable to Gerrit.

Ann did consistently maintain a positive attitude toward moral reform. "What a trifle it takes to make us happy when we are right minded," she said. She set the tone of optimism that pervaded the house. One family friend referred to Ann as

> "warm-hearted and affectionate, sympathetic with all [of Gerrit's] sentiments, ideas, and purposes, a moral and spiritual cooperator, delicate of constitution and poetic in temperament, [she] diffused an air of cheerful serenity over the household."

Another described her as

> "...a noble woman... blessed with a mild, frank face, the index of a pure and generous nature. Her dark liquid eyes have an expression of tenderness which wins your confidence and affection at a glance; and then her voice is soft and musical, and her manner so utterly devoid of affectation, one cannot look at her without loving her."[9]

Ann had a deep capacity for sympathizing with what Gerrit called "down-trodden and oppressed" people. In 1844, she administered a large dinner at her house at which forty people of diverse social classes attended, after which she commented,

> "I fear the presence of the poor caused separation.... I feel more and more the necessity + joy of identifying ourselves with the poorest of the poor."[10]

Although she had a philanthropic heart, she controlled few resources that she could use to express generosity. Only late in her life did Gerrit allow her to have a bank account of her own that she could disburse as she wished. And when she could do that, it was her habit to walk around the hamlet of Peterboro to visit with residents, determine their needs, and supply them with cash. Even so, her main focus for teaching moral behavior was her family.

Ann and Gerrit had a total of seven children between 1822 and 1842, only two of whom lived to adulthood. Three of their children died in infancy, one at age five, and one at age twelve. Their firstborn, Elizabeth, lived to age 89, and Greene only until age 38. But their empathy with other extended family members led them to board and raise, at least temporarily, eleven other children.

A Peterboro Street Scene in 1907, looking north from the village green. Most storefronts remained unchanged since Gerrit Smith's days in the 1800s.

From the author's collection

When Gerrit's older sister Cornelia Smith Cochrane died early in her life, Gerrit and Ann agreed to keep her eight children at their Peterboro home for three years so that her husband could have time to adjust to a new lifestyle. Later during other family emergencies, they helped raise two of one of Ann's sister's children, and one child of Gerrit's brother.

One aspect of their home life that drew accolades of praise from visitors was Ann and Gerrit's joint effort at hospitality. This is an important point regarding the reform era because the Smith home was a center for recruitment. People who came there received information about reform ideas, encouragement to participate however they could in accordance with their personal resources, and assurance that their talents would be appreciated and respected.

The hamlet of Peterboro might seem to be an unusual place to be of central importance to national social movements unless one considers the significance of Gerrit and Ann Smith's presence there. Because of their philanthropic attitude combined with their abundant financial resource, Peterboro became a magnet for all kinds of unconventional causes and people—a Mecca for those seeking any kind of help.

Business Directory of Peterboro

MISS CELINDA H. MARSH,
—FASHIONABLE DRESSMAKER.—
Rooms at residence opposite Evans Academy.

MRS. EMMA C. R. CRAMER,
Teacher of
—DRAWING, CRAYONING & PAINTING.—

D. ELLIS COLE,
—POPULAR BILLIARD PARLOR.—
Fresh Ales and Lager constantly on hand; also Oysters, Clams, Bolognas and other eatables.

W. H. JOHNSON,
—TINNER,—
Rooms over Cameron's meat market. Repairing of all kinds promptly done.

DR. F. E. DEWEY,
—PHYSICIAN & SURGEON,—
Peterboro, N. Y.
Office at residence, corner of Main and Mill Streets.

C. E. CAMERON,
Sells the juiciest STEAK, fattest PORK, plumpest FOWLS, largest OYSTERS and [illegible] any dealer in Madison County.

J. G. MARSH,
—UNDERTAKING—
in all its branches skillfully performed. Bodies cared for and embalmed. Good Hearses, Carriages and Flowers furnished to order.

DUANE W. COE,
Calls attention of all farmers to the fact that he is a breeder of registered
—SHROPSHIRE SHEEP.—
☞ Call and see them.

A. M. BUMP,
Proprietor of the
—PETERBORO MILLS.—
Has everything desired in the line of Mill Stuffs. Superior grade of Buckwheat Flour constantly on hand.

MRS. C. E. CAMERON,
has Home-made BREAD, PIES, CAKES, COOKIES, DOUGHNUTS, and everything pertaining to a first-class bakery constantly on hand.

W. EMMETT COE,
Drugs and Medicines,
FINE SOAPS, PERFUMERY,
TOILET & FANCY GOODS,
Pure Wines and Liquors; Fine line of Groceries.

S. TRANAHAN DOWNER,
—DEPUTY SHERIFF.—

MISS MARY WILBER,
—DRESSMAKING—
in all its branches skillfully performed.

WM. McPHERSON,
—CARPENTER, JOINER & BUILDER.—
First-class work guaranteed.

MRS. WM. McPHERSON,
—FASHIONABLE DRESSMAKER.—
Rooms at residence, first door east of hotel.

J. N. WOODBURY,
—NOTARY PUBLIC—
and General Conveyancer.

GEO. W. COE,
—JUSTICE OF THE PEACE—
and General Conveyancer.

DAVID DEVAN,
—WAGON MAKER,—
Repairing promptly done and in a workman-like manner.

EDWARD BLISS,
—NOTARY PUBLIC,—
Office at house. Special care taken in drawing mortgages, contracts, wills, etc.

MISS GERTRUDE HARRINGTON,
—TEACHER OF PIANO & ORGAN.—
Residence corner Main and Hamilton streets. Pupils at a distance, $8 for 20 lessons; at residence, $5.

R. E. TORREY,
—BLACKSMITH.—
All hand-turned work. Horse Shoeing a specialty. Highest cash price paid for all kinds of Fur.

THE FIRM OF
Hecox & Wagoner having mutually agreed to dissolve partnership, which has existed for the past two years, give notice that the creditors are requested to call and settle their accounts within thirty days from this date.

L. H. MARTINDALE,
—Proprietor of—
PETERBORO HOTEL,
Accommodations for man and beast unexcelled in the county. First-class board by the day or week. An A No. 1 quality of Wines and Liquors always on hand; also Ale, Lager and Small Beers.

ALL (REIDY)
To furnish the whole world with
Harnesses, Trunks, Whips,
Traveling Bags, Halters, Combs, Brushes, Hames, Oils, and Horse clothing of all kinds at prices so low that no one can afford to do without. I can back these statements with facts. Come one, come all.
D. S. REIDY.

LEVI MILLER, JR.,
—PRACTICAL CHEESE MAKER,—
at Peterboro, N. Y.

CHARLES OSBORN,
—STEAM SAW MILL,—
Custom Work promptly done.

H. NILES HARRINGTON,
Duly authorized United States claim and Pension Agent. Also Justice of the Peace and conveyancer. Office at residence.

FRANK SHAFER,
—DISTILLER OF ESSENTIAL OILS,—
Also manufacturer of Novelty and Aparian Goods of all kinds.

MRS. W. E. COE,
Dealer in
—FASHIONABLE MILLINERY—
and Fancy Goods.

A. C. HADDEN,
◁ SELLS DRY GOODS, ▷
Groceries, Crockery, Boots and Shoes, Hats and Caps, Ready-made Clothing and everything pertaining to a first-class stock of Gen[eral Merchandise] at prices [illegible]. Call and be convinced.

I. O. WRIGHT,
—Dealer in—
Hardware, Groceries,
Crockery, Glassware, Tinware, Agricultural Implements, Wall Paper, &c. Would call special attention to a fine line of Teas and Coffees. Prices guaranteed. Fifty cent tea at 40 cents. Good Flour, $1.25.

PIANOS & ORGANS.
The best in the market, including the celebrated Ivers & Pond, Hallet & Davis, Wm. Bourn and McCammon Pianos; the uncomparable Wilcox & White, B. Shoninger Organs, and cheaper pianos and organs, all at lowest possible prices for cash or on time. Call on me or write for catalogue and terms before buying.
M. L. DENISON, Peterboro, N. Y.

A list of Peterboro businesses from the late 1800s reveals a thriving period in the history of a small community.

From the author's collection

In the 1830-1860 era, Peterboro was a quiet, isolated, self-sufficient hamlet, seemingly remote from the clash of diverse people and ideas within cities. Its beautiful three-acre village green was surrounded by new residences, thirty-one active businesses, and a human population of approximately four hundred. People lived within walking distance of places of work, schools, churches, service professionals, hotels, and grocery or hardware stores. Life in such a small town flowed peacefully among people who knew each other, and were deeply infused with a sense of identity in both their function and the place. Pride in being valued for one's expertise characterized the blacksmith, the shoemaker, the tailor, the carpenter, the undertaker, and the butcher. And their local pride in being Peterboro residents was fueled by the national reputation of the Smith family.

Gerrit and Ann liked to help their neighbors feel good, and have a stake in the quality of life in Peterboro. They regularly helped those in financial need and those who were facing a personal or family crisis. At one point in the 1840s, they helped hamlet residents to achieve home

The Smith mansion, looking north from the village green. Despite its grand outer appearance and 28 rooms, the home Peter Smith built was simply appointed inside, in keeping with Gerrit's and Ann's aversion to displays of wealth.

From the author's collection

A view of the Smith mansion, looking west from the east lawn. The well-sculpted walkways and gardens were a favorite among the family's many visitors. At the far right of thr lower photo are the stable and the laundry, two buildings that remain today.

From the author's collection

The Reform Era

ownership by purchasing rented property and donating it to them. Pride in property ownership, they believed, was healthy for village morale.

Because people did not move often, life in mid-nineteenth century Peterboro was stable with a sense of balance among people, animals, functions, and their environment. Simplicity reigned, and time was not cut in slices too thin for thought. People matured to the point of entertaining the possibility of contributing to the development of a social life characterized by justice and equality.

In this idealistic physical and social setting sat what was called "The Smith Mansion," or "The Big House."

Originally the two-story house of Peter and Elizabeth Smith and their four children, it was enlarged in 1854 by Gerrit and Ann. They preferred to have it unostentatious both inside and outside, with no pretensions of wealth or privilege. Even so, it was huge, eventually having twenty-eight rooms inside. There were no elegant carpets, no ornate furniture, no mirrors or drapes. Paintings of friends and some favorite sayings hung on the walls, with a central hallway separating the parlor and conservatory from the kitchen and library.

The paintings and pictures that hung in the house gave one a sense of what was important to Ann and Gerrit. Family portraits hung in the living room, and included Elizabeth Smith (Miller) and her husband Charles Dudley Miller, Ann and Gerrit, Gerrit's mother Elizabeth Livingston Smith, and Ann's father William Frisby Fitzhugh. In the library hung portraits of leading abolitionists William Lloyd Garrison, John Brown, Charles Sumner, Wendell Phillips, and Frederick Douglass.

In the central hallway hung a painting of a pastoral nature with cows, sheep, goats, a man doing the milking, and a milk-maid carrying a pail.[14]

Outside in the surrounding yard were various types of shrubbery, flowers, and trees, a vegetable garden, a fountain, and several gravel paths connecting the house to the gardens and other buildings.

While Gerrit and Ann lived there, they had no electricity or telephone, but such "comforts" were not necessary for them to offer a brand of splendid hospitality to all who visited. The testimony of visitors accentuates the significance of feeling like you belong there as a part of the ongoing process of moral reform. The Smith household, visitors claim, was a perfect model of their reform goals.

> While visiting the Smiths, "Miss Putnam" wrote to a friend, "I only wish you could share our visit amid all this exquisite hospitality—the sweet kindness, the freedom that reigns here. This is our second day and I feel already that the visit is going to be one of the pleasantist events of my life."

Her mention of "freedom" here is an enlightening point regarding the ambience of the Smith home and how they made other people feel.

Two important themes are at work here: *Freedom* is the most powerful motivational force, and *feelings* represent a person's sense of respect for and identity with the present source of stimulation.

The burning desire for freedom motivated slaves to risk it all by fleeing, and we can see the same motive operate today as people escape from situations in which they feel trapped. The fact that the Smith home exemplified freedom and presented it to others as an option for themselves, or as a possibility for others who face oppression, is a fact with monumental historical implications and consequences. To encourage others to feel a sense of independence, autonomy, and self-sovereignty is a major thematic goal of the moral reform movement. To be free from control by slave masters, tyrannical husbands, or oppressive governments was the obsession that drove reformers onward in the face of brutal treatment and intense prejudice.

Another visitor remembered

> "the Grand old Mansion where I and my wife enjoyed a few of the most truly happy hours of our lives.... [We] will never forget the baronial hospitality."

One last testimony comes from Edwin Morton, a Harvard classmate of Secret Six member Franklin Benjamin Sanborn, and tutor to Greene Smith at Peterboro. He had lived in the Smith home in the late 1850s while tutoring Greene in preparation for his future attendance at Harvard University. After having left Peterboro, Morton wrote nostalgically to Greene about a pending visit,

"When I get back, I shall long to come up to Peterboro and spend a few days at the old place. You will let me have my old room again, where I can see the sunsets once more, and I will try once more the familiar rides and drives and walks. I want to be again in 'The Library,' where I met so often with your father, and went over so many 'last papers for the press,' the dining room, scene of so many pleasant talks; and in the parlor in the evening, we would make the music of the years long gone...."

Clearly, the impression the Smiths made on others was powerful and long-lasting, and was an important tool in mustering help for their reform goals.[11]

A corollary aspect of their hospitality was the constant flow of unannounced visitors. Ann wrote to Bess, Greene's wife, "Since last Tuesday (five days ago) we have had twenty visitors. Three staid all night, 15 ate with us, and the rest were calls." Elizabeth kept track of visitors to the Peterboro mansion for fourteen months during 1841-1842, and recorded an average of thirty-three visitors per month. Ann commented in a letter to Elizabeth, "I wanted to write to you before this, but we have had so many coming and going that I have found no time."[12]

Between 1842 and 1853, the Smith family lived at "The Grove," a small house one mile south of Peterboro, in order to save money during an economic depression. Even while living there, they still had many visitors. According to one who spent several days there, the place was "unostentatious" to the extent that there was no place in the house where "the most humble human being" would not feel comfortable. The home exhibited

"an upward-soaring spirit, bursting the fetters of selfishness and materialism,... a spirit that no caste or color... nor power of silver or gold can... jostle form the orbit of a genuine and universal love."

The Smiths, this visitor said, "feel a very close and tender sympathy with poverty and its sufferings, [and] an intuitive appreciation of the pains and trials of the hundreds of poor people...."[13]

A striking aspect of the parade of visitors to the Smith home was their extensive social diversity. According to a report in the New York Times, the Peterboro mansion was a welcoming place where "visitors were of the most miscellaneous and amusing description. They included aristocrats attracted to Peterboro as a restful resort, poor people looking for help, inventors seeking financial support for strange ideas, fugitive slaves headed north, Native Americans on relief efforts, and reformers of all sorts."

And, due to the benevolence of the Smiths, "they were never sent away empty."[15]

Gerrit's brother-in-law Frederick F. Backus, a respected medical doctor, wrote to Gerrit about an issue that concerned him that he had learned about in the Rochester newspapers: "We hear much said in the public prints of Mr. + Mrs. Smith having diverse negroes at their dining table."

For people with racist attitudes, this was a crucial matter that could cause much distress. People who lived outside of Peterboro often had difficulty understanding the truly integrated quality of that community.

Due to the influence of the Smiths, interracial activity was accepted and common there. Black and white people ate together, worked together, played, and worshipped together. At times, Gerrit and Ann had white visitors refuse to eat at the same table with black people. The Smiths were only expressing their own beliefs, and setting an example that they hoped would spread.[16]

Gerrit's first biographer had for his use Gerrit's 400-page diary, a marvelous resource that was probably destroyed in the 1936 fire that demolished the Smith mansion. In the diary, Gerrit had recorded some visits that indicate the array of people arriving:

"A man calling himself George Brown, of Corning, comes here to-night with a very heavy pack on his back. He is accompanied by his wife and child. The child is deaf."

"Mrs. Crampton, a beggar woman, spent last night with us. Charles Johnson, a fugitive slave from Hagerstown, took tea at our house last evening and breakfasted with us this morning."
"Mr. William Corning, a wandering pilgrim, as he styles himself, dines with us. He is peddling his own printed productions."
"Peter Johnson, a colored, illiterate man, calling himself a missionary, arrives this afternoon. He has been among the colored people in Canada, and is going to Hayti."

"Mrs. Phiak of Port Byron, a poor old Dutch woman, arrives. She leaves after breakfast. A begging blind man, and a begging woman and her son from Cazenovia breakfast at our house."
"Poor Graham, the insane literary colored man, has been with us a day or two."

"William Henry Douglass, of Paterson, New Jersey, son of Aaron Douglass, comes to our house this morning. Says he is nineteen years old, and ran away from his home a week ago last Saturday. He has been to Buffalo, repent of his folly, and is on his return home. He has no money. I gave him three dollars and some bread and cheese. He breakfasts with us, and starts for home."

"Elder Cook and William Haines of Oneida depot arrive this evening. Mr. H. is a 'medium,' and speaks in unknown tongues."
"Dr. Winmer of Washington City, with five deaf mutes and a blind child take supper and spend the evening with us."

"We find Brother Swift and wife and daughter at our house, where they will remain until they get lodgings. There come this evening an old black man, a young one and his wife and infant.

They say that they are fugitives from North Carolina."

"A man from [illegible] brings his mother, six children and her half sister, all fugitives from Virginia."

"An Indian and a fugitive slave spent last night with us. The Indian has gone on, but Tommy McElligott (very drunk) has come to fill his place."[17]

From the daily journal of Elizabeth Smith's tutor, Caroline King, comes the following: Gerrit had picked up a drunk man on the road as he traveled to Peterboro from Morrisville. Caroline noted that "he now lies on a buffalo robe by the fire." On another occasion, she wrote, "A poor, wandering woman who sings hymns and talks continually" arrived at the Smith home. "She is given a room, made comfortable, and allowed to stay for a week." Obviously, the Smiths' hospitality extended to all.[18]

In June of 1859, Gerrit's friend George Thomas dined with the Smiths in Peterboro and remarked,

"I was most courteously received and hospitably entertained. Had I been a duke or dutchess, president or potentate, I could not have expected or desired to have met with a more cordial reception, or to be treated with more kind attention and regard. I have reason to believe that the black fugitive slave from the South met with a warmer reception and a more kindly greeting at the home of Mr. Smith than myself or any of the more favored of any race."[19]

Another important feature of the Smiths' hospitality involved how they treated other participants in the reform movement, especially those who were also recognized as national leaders. The bonds among reformers were strong, reflecting the social hazards they all faced. Their mutual reinforcement of efforts to spread the moral reform message strengthened their resolve to carry on in spite of public opposition. When they met with one another, their conversation harbored a group therapy function. They wanted to visit with each other to recharge their internal batteries in preparation for the next chapter of the crusade, and the Smiths' home became a comfortable retreat for that purpose.

The abolitionists who met there at various times illustrate the significance of mutual revitalization:

- U.S. Senator Charles Sumner of Massachusetts visited in November of 1870. Gerrit noted that "at 3PM my neighbors assembled in front of our piazza and Mr. Sumner spoke to them for upward of an hour."[20]
- Horace Greeley, editor of the New York Tribune.
- John Brown, leader of the Harpers Ferry invasion.
- Salmon P. Chase, U.S. senator and governor of Ohio; Chief Justice of the United States.
- William Lloyd Garrison, leader of the "Boston clique" of abolitionists.
- Frederick Douglass, escaped slave and newspaper editor.
- James G. Birney, former slaveholder turned abolitionist; Liberty Party candidate for president.
- John Greenleaf Whittier, poet and abolitionist.
- Elizabeth Cady Stanton, leader of the women's rights movement.
- Susan B. Anthony, leader of the women's rights movement.

These are just a few of the leaders of the moral reform era, and they all knew and loved to visit with Gerrit and Ann Smith at Peterboro.

Two other important Smith family players in the reform era will be covered in later chapters which deal with specific issue areas. Elizabeth Smith Miller and Gerrit's first cousin Elizabeth Cady Stanton will be prominent in the chapter on women's rights.

To conclude this chapter on the reform era, we must note something important about its aftermath. For approximately one hundred years following the Civil War and the ratification of the human rights-oriented thirteenth, fourteenth, and fifteenth amendments to the United States Constitution, the themes and messages of the reformers regarding prejudice, empathy, and the drive to achieve justice and equity in the treatment of all persons waned. The racial scene was poisoned with reactionary "Jim Crow" laws that intentionally legitimated and institutionalized discrimination against black people, and the women's rights movement—especially the pursual of woman suffrage—was ignored by male-dominated state and national legislatures.

This hiatus in public passion that previously favored the recognition of natural rights in all persons, and the dedication to implementing equitable treatment of all persons, nearly halted progress in human rights issues throughout the United States—including Peterboro! Why this happened is an important social and historical question.

In Peterboro, after Gerrit and Ann Smith died in the mid-1870s, their intense and persistent stimulation of concern for the morality of equality was gone. Without that incitement in constant view, local residents' incentive to continue their human rights work received no guidance, and faded in concert with such attitudes throughout the country.

A major force contributing to this pause in concern for social issues was the rapid advancement of science and reason for thinking about and solving problems instead of reliance on morals and ethics. In the 1850s, people were finding greater motivational and problem-solving force in scientific advances instead of relying on supernatural assumptions. Emerging scientific facts were rational, easy to understand, and made life predictable and controllable. One no longer needed to turn to gods and religion for explanations of complex social or natural events. Rather than focus on moralistic reformers to advance the elimination of selfishness and individualism, people could develop institutions to carry out social welfare-oriented goals.

Sources of authority for guiding social behavior switched from reformers and religious leaders to scientists and self-empowered individuals. In this new progressive era, reason replaced superstition, thereby diluting the ethical force of commandments and miracles. This shift in the mental orientation to life that caused concern for

Greene Smith (at right in left photo with friend Hiram Wilson and in a portrait in right photo) led a short and troubled life, but his joy was the outdoors and, eventually, a love for preserving birds of all kinds in the special 'Birdhouse' Gerrit had built for him close to the Smith mansion.

Photos from the author's collection

---

human rights to take a back seat is personified superbly in the life of Ann and Gerrit's son, Greene Smith.

Born on April 14, 1842, Greene was the Smiths' last child. Having lost five of their seven children previously, Ann and Gerrit must have wondered if they were setting themselves up for another heartbreak. In a way, they were, but it would not be due to Greene's death. He was named in honor of Gerrit's admired abolitionist friend Beriah Green, and as a very young boy, displayed traits of independence and rebelliousness.[21]

The focus of Greene's boyhood interests was the outdoor, natural world. Whereas Gerrit wanted to groom the boy to become the manager of the land sale business, Greene showed no interest in that, and wanted to be outside. At a very young age, he developed an obsession with birds that would become his life's work.

Fishing and hunting became favorite activities for Greene in his preteen years. Gerrit viewed these recreational pursuits as a waste of time, and actually wrote a business-like contract with Greene to stop his son from doing them and to instead develop economically productive projects. Greene rebelled against his father, and remained remote from him for the rest of his life.

At age nine, Greene was sent away from his beloved Peterboro to a school for moral training operated by Gerrit's abolitionist friends Theodore Dwight Weld and Angelina Grimké in Belleville, New Jersey. Greene resented this move, and detested the school which took him away from what he loved to do.

When he reached his teenage years, his love of birds had matured into the intent to build a collection of mounted birds for scientific study. In the mid-1800s, the preferred technique of studying animal species was to mount them as museum specimens. This encouraged public interest in observing them, and hopefully learning about natural ecosystems. The emergence of industrialization gave some impetus to its opposite, the study of the complexity of ecosystems, so this trend toward public interest in species variety was believed to be a first step toward protection. Greene liked that idea and became deeply involved in bird study.

Greene learned the science and art of taxidermy by studying and training with John Graham Bell of Tappan, New York. Bell was an accomplished taxidermist and an associate of John James Audubon. Audubon died in 1851 when Greene was nine years old, so it is unlikely that they knew each other, but Greene became a well-known ornithologist and was very familiar with Audubon's works.

Greene also studied taxidermy with Spencer F. Baird of the Smithsonian Institution, and Elliot Coues, whose publication <u>Field Ornithology</u> was Greene's guide to species collection.

Greene collected bird species by shooting birds and then mounting them for display. He did so well at it that many of his original specimens still exist in fine condition. The taxidermy process used chemical poisons like arsenic to preserve the birds, and the hazardous work may have contributed to Greene's death at age thirty-eight in 1880.

To display his collection of over three thousand birds, eggs, and nests, he built in 1863 a "Birdhouse" of elegant construction. It was

Above: The Birdhouse, which Greene Smith built in 1863 with an outer facade of hemlock bark, featured a grand mahogany staircase and 77 walnut display cases. The building had a downstairs fountain and indoor pond that was home to living fish and waterfowl. Next page: This rare surviving interior photo shows just a portion of the immense collection of birds and other animals Greene displayed, mostly from hunting. After Greene died from tuberculosis in 1880 at the age of 38, the collection was gradually removed from the building and the Birdhouse fell into disrepair.

From the author's collection

---

two stories high with a central mahogany staircase that led to an upper mezzanine area. Seventy-seven glass-covered walnut cases protected many of the mounted birds. A running water fountain contained live fish and water birds, and some live birds flew around inside large caged areas. The outside of the Birdhouse was covered with hemlock bark, giving it a natural and rustic look.

The 1850s were an exciting time of emerging scientific discoveries regarding the natural world. Ecosystems shed their mystery as having been created simply by an omnipresent, powerful god. New information proved that the earth was much older than ten thousand years, and that species of animals and plants were in flux and changing constantly, rather than static representations of a supernatural creative force.

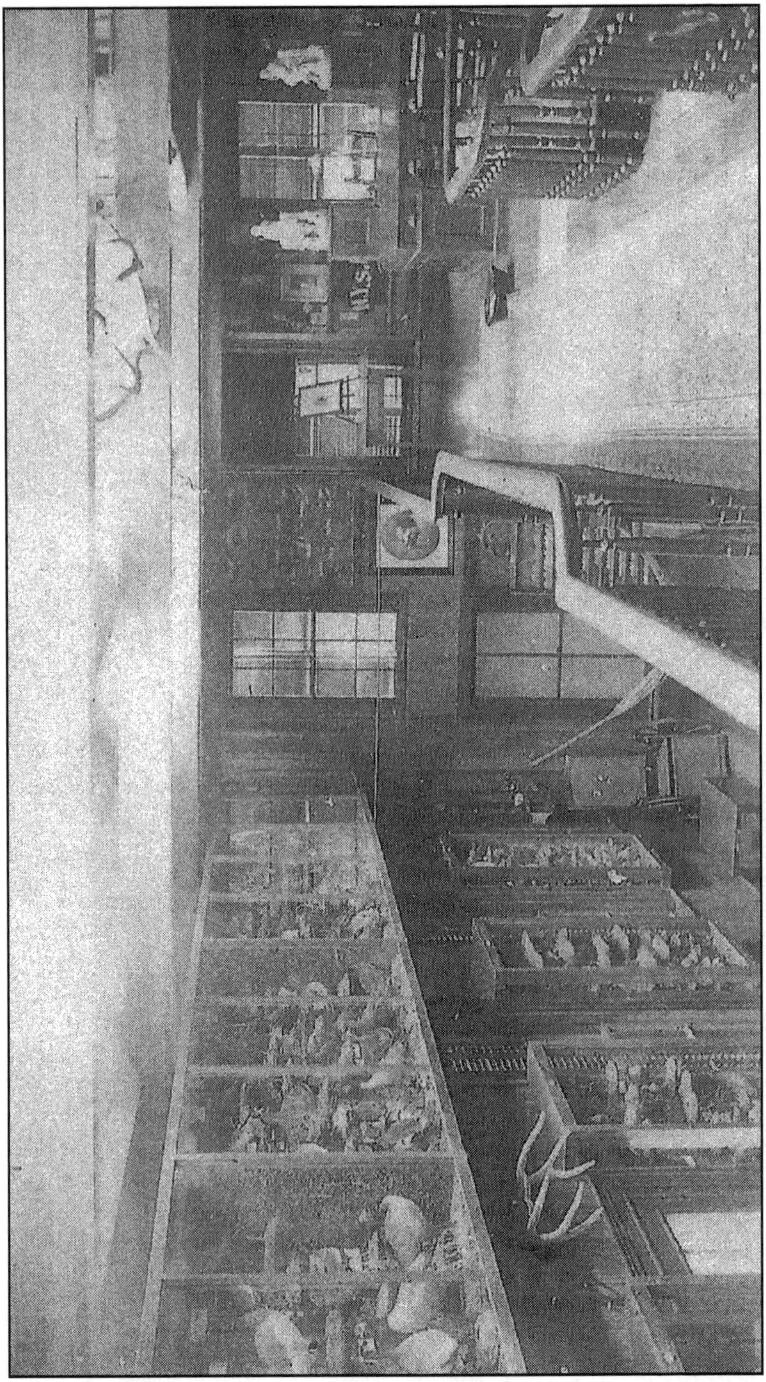

The work that epitomized such new learning was Charles Darwin's book "On The Origin of Species," published in 1859. In it, he summarized over twenty years of research that supported the notion that all living species of both plants and animals had evolved over many millions of years to adapt to specific environmental conditions by means of the process of natural selection. This idea was well received in the scientific community, and supported by similar work done by other researchers.

These facts demolished long accepted and highly authoritative religious explanations of the origin of the earth and its living species. This serious challenge of traditional authority is a single, but illustrative example of the loss of power by conventional power brokers who for thousands of years had successfully maintained their authoritative position and controlled the public mind through superstition. Scientists were iconoclasts breaking down long-standing sources of influence and rule, thereby empowering critically thinking individuals to make their own decisions, and self-actualize their own desires. This is precisely what Greene Smith did.

Greene became a self-educated citizen-scientist; that is, he did not have formal academic training, but pursued his obsessions independently, seeking out the experts in developing scientific fields and studying their works either directly with them, or indirectly through reading. The result was that he rebelled not only against the overbearing authority of his family, but also against the well-accepted social authority figures like priests, teachers, and business leaders.

Greene's rebellion did not prevent his success because the cultural trends saw value in scientific research, embraced new ideas, and were tired of the moralistic reformers' demands.

The fact that Greene Smith existed within the bosom of a dedicated moral reform family demonstrates the clash of ideas at the junction of the reform and industrial eras, and beautifully symbolizes the role played by the Smith family during the reform era.

They were trapped—as we all are in some sense—by predominating cultural norms and expectations. In the early decades of reform,

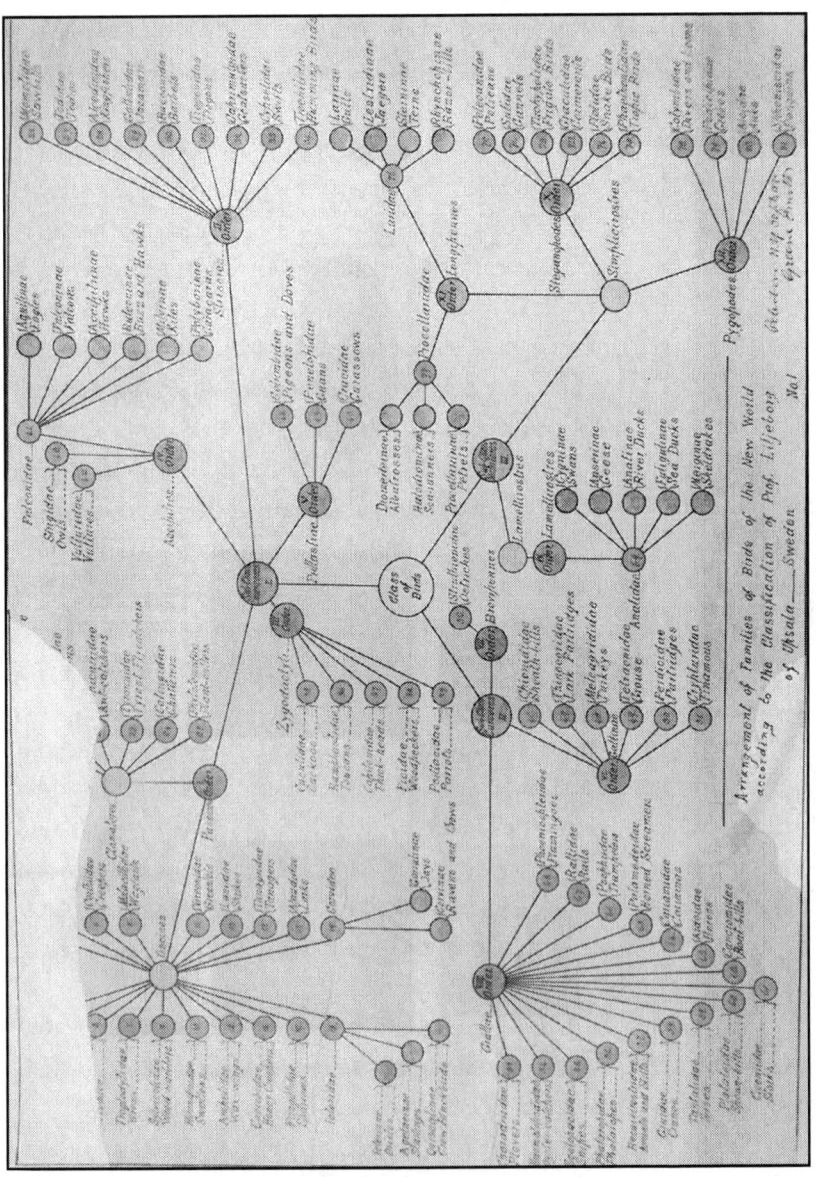

Along with his extensive collection of birds, eggs and related materials, Greene Smith made a huge contribution to the emerging study of ornithology with taxonomic charts of bird species. As shown on these two pages, Smith arranged the charts as family genealogies to make them easier to understand. Following page: Smith explained the charts and acknowledged the source of the data as being a Swedish professor. *From the author's collection*

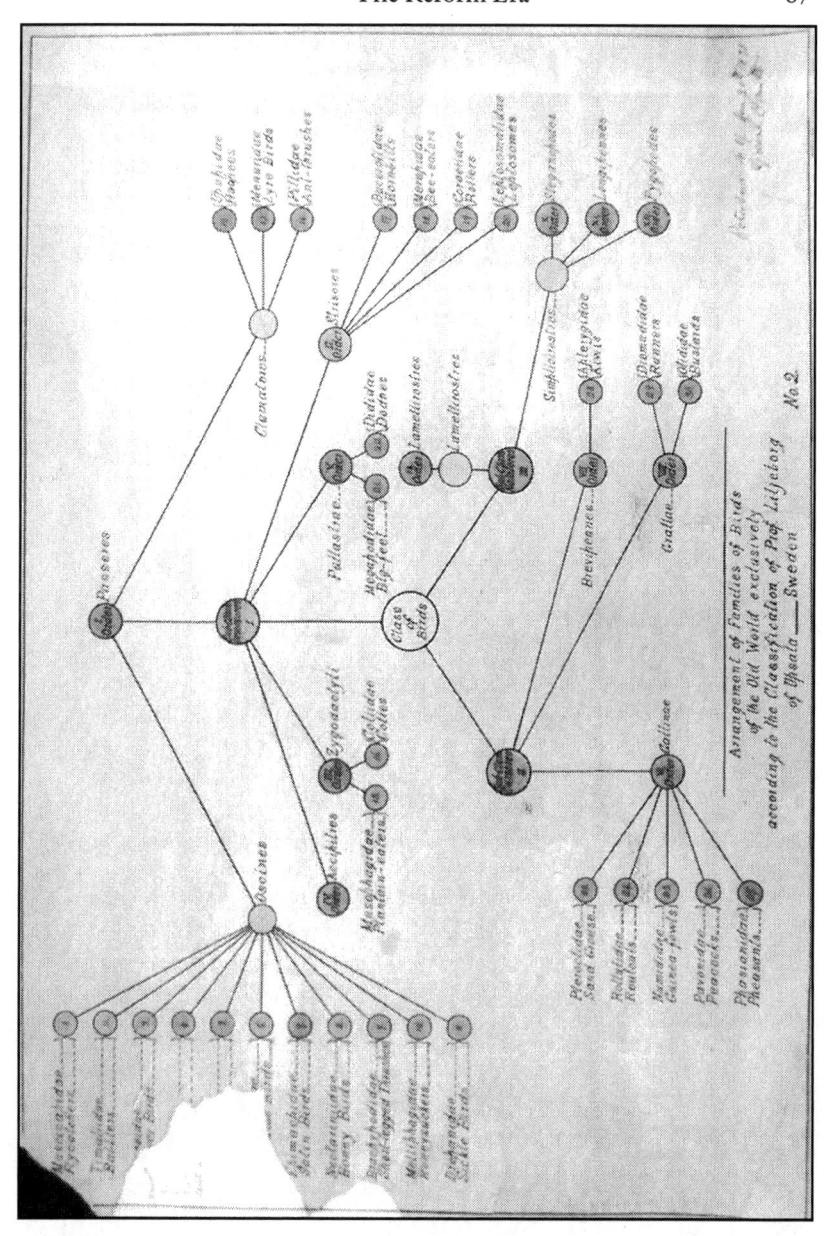

The Reform Era

This method of classification, now adopted provisionally, by the Smithsonian Institute at Washington, is that of Professor Liljeborg of Upsala, Sweden, and is based on the theory of progression.

I am indebted to Professor S. F. Baird, of the Smithsonian, for kindly furnishing me with a paper descriptive of this arrangement of the families of birds, which I have placed on charts that it may, perhaps, be more understandable to students of Ornithology.

A tree of genealogy is familiar to almost every one, and these charts are based upon the same principle.

Observing the center of either chart, the white circle represents the CLASS OF BIRDS. Then, following the lines to the smaller circles, we come to the divisions and sub-divisions of the CLASS as far as the FAMILIES and SUB-FAMILIES.*

The dark green circles represent SUB-CLASSES, the purple ORDERS, the ochre-yellow SECTIONS, the carmine FAMILIES, and the emerald-green SUB-FAMILIES.

The Roman numbers in the circles representing ORDERS indicate the steps of progression, Order XII being the lowest, and Order I being the highest in the CLASS OF BIRDS. The Arabic numbers in the circles representing FAMILIES indicate, in a like manner, the steps of progression. For instance: the *Penguins* on chart No. 1, *family* 81, have no song, are utterly unable to fly, and walk with difficulty, while on the same chart the *Thrushes*, *family* 1, are fine singers, expert on the wing, in running, walking and perching.

Should this method of representing the classification of Birds on charts prove to be of service to those studying this branch of natural science, I intend to make from time to time similar charts, representing the *sub-divisions* of the *families* into *genera*, *sub-genera*, and *species*.

GREENE SMITH.

PETERBORO, N. Y., Jan. 20th, 1871.

b 2

* On Chart No. 1, I have followed Prof. Liljeborg in making the *orders* of the NATATORES sub-divisions of *sections*, whilst it makes the *sections* OSCINES and CLAMATORES sub-divisions of the *order* PASSERES.

they conformed to the religious model, but as time progressed, they became more secular in their approach to achieving human rights goals. It is the successful maturation of Greene into the scientific world that so clearly illustrates the forces at work.

Greene's fascination with the study of birds also led him into a corollary endeavor—sportsmanship. He enjoyed many hunting and fishing expeditions, as well as competitive efforts in shooting. He became a national champion at trapshooting, winning many ribbons, medals, and trophies that he proudly displayed in his Birdhouse. In the 1870s, he served as president of sportsmens" associations at the county, state, and national levels, and proposed the first laws for the protection of fish and game that were enacted by the New York State Legislature. He also developed the first set of taxonomic charts of species of birds. They were adopted by Cornell University for educational purposes in its fledgling ornithology program, in which Greene presented lectures in June 1870.

As a successful and nationally recognized citizen-scientist by the late 1870s, Greene was headed toward a career of major significance in emerging science fields. The tragedy is that medical science had not yet advanced enough by 1880 to prevent his death due to tuberculosis. The significance of his life in the contents of this book is its illustration of the forces of change operating both in the Smith family and in the larger culture.

A fascinating addendum to this story of the reform era in Peterboro and its ensuing one-hundred-year hiatus rests in the sequence of events that ended it in the 1960s and 1970s. After the second World War, a new generation matured into young adulthood in the mid-1960s. Affluence and expanding opportunities for higher education combined to sensitize many to the ongoing discrimination against minorities—especially African-Americans. When those victims of discrimination rebelled in the urban riots of that decade, liberal-minded people responded with the demand for civil rights legislation. Thus, the old abolitionist passion for natural and equal human rights was reignited.

In the hamlet of Peterboro, with about one-half the population that it had in the 1850s, Rev. Robert Rowe inaugurated an historically-oriented "Old Home Day" to commemorate the role of Peterboro in fostering concern about human rights issues. This incentive lead in 1975 to the creation of the Peterboro Area Historical Society on August 20 by a small group of local people, probably inspired by both Peterboro's past, and the growing concern for civil rights. In respect to all of them, I include here the full list of charter members:

Thomas Anderson
Harriet and Maurice Blackman
Mary Brown
John and Martha Campbell
Mildred Davis
Carl and Ximena DeGroat
Donna Dorrance
James and Maud[e] Dorrance
Mary Dorrance
Seymour and Sylvia Ellis
Carl Frank
Doris Hall
Donald and Joan Huller
Ginnia and Taze Huntley
Leon Judd
Bessie Langberg
Jack Miller
Minnie Munderback
Downer and Marjorie Packwood
Jan and John Sebring
Molly and Myron Smith
Margaret Stewart
Margaret Stoker
Mildred and Walter Tucker, Sr.
James and Ellen Williams
Arthur and Olive Williams

Interestingly, this author was not involved in Peterboro history at that time in 1975, but Taze Huntley was my officemate in the Social Science Department at Morrisville State College, just six miles from Peterboro. I clearly remember Taze telling me in August of 1975 that a new historical society had been formed in Peterboro.

This organization has been active since its inception, and, through the work of its original and subsequent members, has spawned other local and national organizations that currently pursue progress in human rights issues.

The Smithfield Community Association was founded in 1991 in Peterboro for the purpose of rehabilitating historic buildings in the hamlet. The SCA worked to establish the property and buildings of the former residence of the Smith family as a place of significance in the nineteenth-century human rights movement. The seven-acre site was added to the National Register of Historic Places in November of 1997, and was recognized by the United States Department of the Interior as a National Historic Landmark in 2001.

The SCA also spawned the National Abolition Hall of Fame and Museum in 2004. Nineteenth century abolitionists are inducted

The site of the National Abolition Hall of Fame and Museum has a long history, first built in 1820 as the Peterboro Presbyterian Church and later home to the Evans Academy. *From the author's collection*

into the Hall of Fame regularly, with nominations open to the public. It is housed in the former Peterboro Presbyterian Church building, built in 1820, and listed on the National Register of Historic Places in 1994. It was the site of the inaugural meeting of the New York State Anti-Slavery Society in October of 1835. A portion of NAHOF's current mission statement reads: it "strives to complete the second and ongoing abolition—the moral conviction to end racism."

Gerrit and Ann Smith would certainly be proud of this new organization that pledges to carry on what they recognized as the moral duty of every citizen—the pursuit of equity in the treatment of all persons.

PART II

The Participation of the Gerrit and Ann Smith Family in Nineteenth-Century Reform Movements

~ 3 ~

The Abolition of Slavery

"The prolonged slavery of woman is the darkest page in human history."

So said Elizabeth Cady Stanton, one of the most influential of the reformers of the roughly 1830-1865 era. She wrote this in 1889 as the first sentence of volume one of her co-authored, six-volume work titled "History of Woman Suffrage."

This powerful statement attracts one's attention instantly to the intensity of discrimination exercised against two categories of people. Stanton equated slaves and women as recipients of the unfair, hypocritical, and bigoted treatment dispensed in United States culture by white males. The population of the United States in 1860 consisted of 13.8 million white males, 13.1 million white females, and 4 million black slaves. This picture shows a minority of 13.8 million discriminating against a collective majority of 17.1 million. And this was happening in a culture supposedly founded upon the democratic principles of justice and equality for all.

In that the United States Constitution and the Declaration of Independence were written by white males, what those principles really meant was that there would be justice and equality for all UNLESS you were black or female. No wonder there was a "re-form" movement! Around 1830, some liberal-minded men and women rebelled against what they viewed as the obviously unfair, bigoted, prejudiced, and unethical treatment of black people and women. It was "unfair" because our fundamental, founding documents proclaimed equality of status and equity in treatment; it was "bigoted" because it exhibited narrowminded intolerance; it was "prejudiced" because it pre-judged the quality of persons based on preconceived notions; it was "unethical" because it exposed the unprincipled and immoral intent of one category of people to retain power at the expense of others.

Those families or individuals who were attracted into the effort to reform discriminatory social institutions were generally in their young adulthood, well-educated, and economically secure. They could see clearly the inequitable distribution of power and the pain it produced for those not white and male. If they possessed what we are now calling the "caring gene," and had time and resources available, they might become reformers, or at least become involved at some level in the reform movement. The Gerrit and Ann Smith family fit this model well. By 1818, Gerrit had completed a four-year college degree in classical letters at Hamilton College in Clinton, New York, and was affluent due to his father Peter's success in building a land sales business. Ann married into this elevated status position in 1822, and, over time, adopted the interests and principles of her husband.

Mainly through the influence and leadership of Gerrit, the family was involved in an amazing variety of reform issues such as diet change, temperance in the consumption of alcohol, opposition to secret societies, religious denomination reform, dress reform, black suffrage, woman suffrage, the abolition of slavery, women's rights, and opposition to the use of tobacco. And that does not exhaust the list. When they got involved with a reform issue, the Smiths exhibited an uncommon degree of fervor, passion, and persistence in their pursual of goals. And this was in spite of the risks involved. They were often vilified in the press for daring to challenge well-established and entrenched norms. Their reputation and, at times, their physical wellbeing was threatened by those who were against the proposed changes.

The name-calling against them was so frequent that they got used to being labeled as "crazy" people.

Among the community of reformers, the Smiths were very well-known and highly respected. They were sought out for advice and inspiration, as well as for financial support for a huge array of causes.

Their ability to lubricate the wheels of reform with their money made them perhaps the most powerful reform family in the nation. They had the one resource that everyone else needed, no matter what cause they championed, so the parade of funding-seekers passed through Peterboro constantly, and most were not disappointed.

The position and influence of the Smith family in the reform era in general, and with respect to specific reform movements within that era, can be traced through their participation in three persistent issue areas: the abolition of slavery, women's rights, and temperance.

In the context of reform-era philosophy and politics, slavery was viewed as an outrageous, flagrant crime. It insulted fundamental democratic principles and Christian virtue. When reformers who were called abolitionists brought the issue out of the backstage shadows and into frontstage glare of reality, nearly *everyone* felt threatened. Southerners obviously opposed the abolition of slavery because they knew that its success would terminate their culture. Most northerners who opposed it did so because they were either benefiting from its huge profits economically, or felt threatened by the potential competition with people whom they were certain were inferior in many ways.

Those in the North who did not favor slavery were mostly indifferent toward it, a point which highlights the difference between an anti-slavery person and an abolitionist.

One could believe that slavery was unjust and a bad idea, and never do anything about it. That would be an anti-slavery person. An abolitionist, however, would work actively to end slavery. They saw the "peculiar institution" of slavery as evil personified, and dedicated their lives to its eradication. Their intensity of commitment to that cause is difficult for most people to understand.

Would you be willing to risk your home (Frederick Douglass' house was burned), your property (James G Birney's printing presses were destroyed more than once), your family's safety (William Lloyd Garrison's wife and children were threatened), and your life (Elijah Lovejoy was killed), for the possible benefit of someone you did not even know? Would you risk being physically beaten because you spoke in public in favor of abolition? (Theodore Dwight Weld was beaten over 150 times for daring to do that.)

Being recognized as an abolitionist—even in the North—was dangerous and hazardous. And those who most actively opposed abolitionists were not social thugs or misfits, but businessmen and politicians—men of "property and standing." It may seem odd that the elite persons of a community would lead the opposition to abolition, but they were the ones who had the largest stake in its profits. Bankers and businessmen often had investments in southern property, or were dependent for supplies on the cheap products of slave labor. Politicians dared not oppose it because so many of their constituents were at least mildly supportive of slavery.

Even amid this confusing complex of values and risks, three members of the Smith family were staunch, steadfast, and unwavering abolitionists. They were Ann, Gerrit, and Elizabeth. Peter, Gerrit's father, was openly racist. He chastised his son for risking public disapproval because of his attitude toward slavery, and condemned him for opening a school for young black males in Peterboro in 1834.

Gerrit disliked his father, calling him a "cold and repulsive" person. Peter's main interest was economic profit for himself. He expressed little empathy for or comprehension of other people. Perhaps Gerrit's empathic and philanthropic attitude was in part reactionary.[1]

Gerrit's commitment to doing something about slavery developed while he was in college, and was first expressed in the 1820s by his support of the American Colonization Society. Because the active phase of the abolition movement did not ignite until 1830, the ACS was one of the few options available to those wishing to help slaves. Its mission was to send free African-Americans back to Africa. Blacks themselves recognized this as a racist goal and opposed the society's work. Gerrit eventually saw this also, but not before donating ten thousand dollars to its cause.

After William Lloyd Garrison started advocating immediate abolition of the entire institution of slavery through this newspaper <u>The Liberator</u> in January of 1831, Gerrit saw the reasonableness of that position, and dropped out of the ACS. In a letter to an abolitionist colleague, Gerrit stated his position clearly:

"[Slavery] at the hearth of Franklin! No! No!! No!!!... Can there be any incongruity more monstrous?... Liberty bearing a chain! Blasphemy echoing from the altar! The collar of the negro chained to the pedestal of Washington.... It is impossible.... The light of the Nineteenth Century is alone enough to destroy it."[2]

And in a speech delivered in Peterboro:
"The organizing of a nation at such a time as this on the basis of slavery is an unendurable defiance of the moral sense of the civilized world."[3]

Gerrit joined the active ranks of the abolition movement in October of 1835 after having been thrown out of an abolitionist meeting in Utica by a mob led by United States Congressman Charles Beardsley. At Gerrit's invitation, that meeting to establish the New York State Anti-Slavery Society resumed in Peterboro under his leadership. Other Central New York abolitionists—Beriah Green, for one—were glad to have Gerrit join them for many reasons, but probably his financial resource was primary.

Smith was elected to the presidency of the NYSASS in 1836, and attended several antislavery conventions in the following years of the 1830s. Ann also became involved in abolition work as she hosted many participants at their Peterboro home. In 1837, she attended the first Antislavery Convention of American Women in New York City, and was selected as one of its vice presidents.

During the last four years of the 1830s, the technique that Gerrit used to pursue abolition was moral suasion. Essentially, it was a form of preaching about the sin of slavery, with the expectation that slave owners would see the immorality of owning people once it was pointed out to them, and voluntarily opt out of slave ownership. That hope reflects both the optimism and the naïveté of abolitionists. They did not at first realize the high intensity of the bias and discrimination that characterized the thought and actions of slave owners.

It was the Garrisonian school of abolitionists in the Boston area that used and advocated the moral suasion technique throughout the reform era. Their logic for doing so made sense: we must first change peoples' attitude toward black people and slavery before the public will commit to its elimination. That was a great idea, but it could not work in the face of the intensity of the bias against black people.

A good way to illustrate the positions of the two camps in the battle over slavery is to contrast the ideas of the antislavery abolitionists with those of the proslavery apologists. This can be done effectively within the context of the ideas and actions of the Gerrit and Ann Smith family.

Imagine with me the following scene: The setting is the large parlor of a nineteenth-century country house. The only people present are two middle-aged female servants who bustle about, dusting chairs, straightening pictures on the wall, and arranging papers on a coffee table. The high-ceiling room is softly and pleasantly lighted by the morning sunlight streaming in through the east windows. A bunch of freshly picked flowers adorn the table. On the walls hang portraits of leaders of the abolition movement. Frederick Douglass stares directly at you with a steely, severe glare, seeming to challenge you to join the fight; William Lloyd Garrison gazes dreamily into the distance; John Greenleaf Whittier leans over some papers on a stand-up desk as he writes another poem about the abolition struggle.

Gerrit stands by the front door just outside of the parlor anxiously watching for the arrival of a very special guest. It is the spring of 1855. The incendiary slavery issue has divided the country into separate cultures that behave like enemy countries before battle. What were once just opinions on both sides are close to becoming the rigid stands of war cries.

At 11:15 AM, a horse-drawn carriage circles around the west end of the Peterboro green and enters the driveway of the Smith estate by passing through the iron gate. Gerrit hustles across the columned porch and down the steps, and with a beaming smile and cheerful voice welcomes George Fitzhugh to Peterboro.

George has traveled from Port Royal Virginia, on the east coast just south of Washington, D.C. He and Gerrit have been communicating by mail since late 1850, and are well-aware of the contrast of their opinions about slavery. Gerrit is a radical abolitionist opting for an immediate end to slavery. George is a proslavery apologist, and has written a book in support of slavery. Published in 1854, "Sociology for the South is an elaborate defense of what Fitzhugh calls the "good institution" of slavery. He has sent to Gerrit a copy of his book, and now visits him for the purpose of discussing their opposite perspectives.

Politically, Fitzhugh was an avowed Democrat. Gerrit abhorred the Democratic Party due to its rigid, conservative stand supporting slavery. Gerrit refused to identify himself with any political party, but he held ultra-liberal views on issues of human rights.

Occupationally, Fitzhugh is a lawyer who specializes in criminal cases, and had been employed in the Attorney General's office of President James Buchanan. He also owns slaves and operates as a small planter. Gerrit had sent to him some antislavery literature in 1852 that prompted Fitzhugh to want to learn more about that set of ideas. He asked Gerrit, "Can any means be devised to ally the growing hostility of the races? This is a practical question." He was evidently concerned about the explosive potential on both sides of the issue, and wanted to discuss the practical aspects of a solution with Gerrit.

Gerrit was also a practical thinker, and thought it to be a good idea to invite Fitzhugh to Peterboro. Gerrit believed that the lack of liberty for anyone would destroy liberty for all. Fitzhugh viewed free society as a pernicious aberration within which

> "Free Negroes and Bloomers disturb the peace of society, threaten the security of property, offend the public sense of decency, assail religion, and invoke anarchy."

Obviously, these two men would have a lot to talk about in the parlor. Learning about their opinions on issues that surround the slavery question is interesting for more than one reason. One obvious point is that in the context of this book, we will see where the influential Smith family stood regarding both the philosophical and practical aspects of the issues. But perhaps more interesting is the fact that because Ann was reared as a Fitzhugh on a slave plantation in the South, Gerrit approached these discussions with George Fitzhugh with an insider's view of both positions. George and Ann Carroll Fitzhugh were distant cousins, having a common ancestor six generations back.

All members of the Smith family had extensive communication with one another, so over the previous decades, the parlor and dinner table talk among Ann, Gerrit, Elizabeth, and Greene had informed each with the thematic ideas on both sides. Visitors to the Smith home often commented on the rich and challenging conversation that characterized the family.

Elizabeth, called Libby, as a young girl held "abolition meetings" with her dolls, and remembered later in life how her parents had instilled their passion in her. She wrote:
"I often think of words they spoke,
Which in our youthful bosoms woke
A fadeless love of Liberty—
A deathless hate of slavery."[4]

No one knows the exact content of the discussions between Gerrit and George, but we can certainly infer with our own creative minds what they might have said. First, we will examine the thought of George Fitzhugh.

Born in November 1806 in eastern Virginia, George had very little formal education. Mainly self-taught as an avid reader, he gained a reputation for public argument as a sarcastic and witty propagandist who supported slavery. His writings did not depend upon political, economic, or legal logic, but upon his personal observations of the social world. Given his absolute proslavery stand, it seems strange that he valued his remote family connections with the abolitionist Gerrit Smith and James Gillespie Birney.

Birney was a former slaveholder who had become an abolitionist, was one of the founders of the Liberty Party, and twice its presidential candidate. He married one of Ann Fitzhugh's sisters. George respected these relatives, and even wanted to hear their opinions regarding slavery. He traveled north only once, and met with Gerrit Smith in Peterboro, and with the Garrisonian abolitionist Wendell Phillips in New Haven, Connecticut.[5]

George claimed that until about 1840, many southerners wondered if slavery was a good idea. Then the abolitionists attempted to flood the South with antislavery literature that vilified slave owners. "We are endeavoring to anticipate them by drenching those materials with ridicule." Because "the abolitionists assailed us," he said, "we looked more closely into our circumstances; became satisfied that slavery was morally right [and] that it was as profitable as it was humane."[6]

Fitzhugh's main point was that free society was a failure. He called it "a violation of the laws of Nature and the revealed will of God." "Free society," he said, "cannot work successfully without a radical change in human nature." He claimed that "Slave society is the only natural society" that can produce social order because "the ordinary relations of men are not competitive and antagonistic as in free society."[7]

The best evidence of this, he claimed, was that the reformers themselves were struggling to change the institutions of free society because of their failure to provide liberty and equality for its subjects. Fitzhugh called the reformers' efforts to change ailing aspects of free society "our trump card." Why would the social leaders of the North need schemes for reform of its institutions if there were no problems? Their proposed remedies exposed the existence of disease. "Abolitionists," Fitzhugh asserted, "had unconsciously discovered and proclaimed the failure of free society long before I did." They evidently believed that "the old, crazy edifice of society in which they live is no longer fit for human dwelling, and is imminently dangerous."[8]

In a letter to William Lloyd Garrison, Fitzhugh asked,
> "Do not all well-informed men of a philosophical turn of mind in the North concur in opinion that the whole framework of society, religious, ethical, economic, legal and political requires radical change?

"Is not the absence of such opinion at the South, and it's prevalence in free society, conclusive proof of the naturalness and necessity of domestic slavery?"[9]

What Fitzhugh did was to deny the value of the traditional American morals of the goodness of human nature, and the humaneness of liberal thinking, optimism, and the innate respectability of all persons. He maintained that the possibility of freedom was a hoax. Because humans are social animals, it is unnatural for them to live alone, so:

> "There is no such thing as <u>natural human</u> liberty." He referred to liberty as "the evil which government is intended to correct. This is the sole object of government.... The question can never arise, who ought to be free? Because no one ought to be free. All government is slavery." Because people group together in social bonds for protection, "liberty is surrendered as the price of security.... Liberty is unattainable, and... not desirable."[10]

What is needed for human survival and happiness, Fitzhugh insisted, was more government control, not less. He noted that "Mobs, secret societies, insurance companies, and... communistic experiments are striking features and characteristics of our day outside of slave society. They are all attempting to supply the defects of regular governments [of free society]." And in the worst case scenario,

> "If ever the abolitionists succeed in thoroughly imbuing the world with their doctrines and opinions, all religion, all government, all order, will be slowly but surely subverted and destroyed."[11]

Obviously, Gerrit Smith disagreed with such opinions. Knowing this, Fitzhugh criticized Smith saying that his

> "charity and benevolence are only exceeded in the greatness of their amount by the grossness of their misapplication. e.g.: He is a Christian, but builds [Free] churches that destroy the ministry;

he is a land monopolist, but gives away land to poor people who cannot manage it; he gives small sums of money to the poor but cannot control its use; he champions freedom yet attempts to reform a failed free society."[12]

Fitzhugh's dissatisfaction and malcontentedness with the abolitionists spilled onto the pages of his book with intense disgust:

"God... in his wisdom has chosen to protect the weak and the poor in a natural and healthy state of society... where domestic slavery exists. Ye meddlesome, profane, presumptuous abolitionists! Think ye that God has done his work imperfectly and needs your aid? Must you steal the negro?... Put your own house in order, ye abolitionists. When the women and children, the sick and the aged, in your laboring class, are secure of the same ample provision, sympathy and attention as our slaves, then, and not until then, offer your advice to us."

"Abolitionists," he claimed, "will make any sacrifice of their time and money to achieve what they think right. They are crazy, no doubt, [and] we would as soon stop a crusader... and prove him the folly of his pursuit, as cure these Abolitionists of their madness."

In a clear act of projection, Fitzhugh believed that "there is not an intelligent reformist... who does not see the necessity of slavery." They all oppose competition and "wish to destroy it. To destroy it is to destroy liberty, and where liberty is destroyed, slavery is established."[13]

Gerrit asked Fitzhugh if the benefits that he insisted were inherent in a slave culture were true, why were there runaways? If, as Fitzhugh stated, "at the South all is peace, quiet, plenty and contentment," why were there slave rebellions? Ironically, Fitzhugh admitted in a letter to a friend, Professor Holmes in 1855, "I see great evils in slavery, but in a controversial work I ought not to admit them."

That statement certainly betrays hypocrisy in his proslavery stand, yet it did not deter him from plodding on in favor of slavery's cruel aspects. And in a letter to Ann Smith, he said, "I admit that negro slavery is the worst form of slavery.... It is simply a necessity."[14]

He viewed slaveowners, "masters," as he called them, as benevolent providers for inept slaves. He faulted free society for attempting through forms of insurance to mimic the "protective, care-taking and supporting feature of slavery. [But] it cannot put a heart and feeling into its... corporations. God makes masters and gives them affections, feelings and interests that secure kindness to the sick, aged and dying slave. Man can never inspire his rickety institutions with those feelings.... The Southerner is the negro's friend, his only friend. Let no intermeddling abolitionist, no refined philosophy dissolve this friendship. [Slavery] begets friendly, kind and affectionate relations, just as equality engenders antagonism and hostility on all sides."

Fitzhugh said that free society has many people who have forfeited their liberty and are, therefore, slaves. Military men, apprentices, the mentally ill, children, and wives all fit that description. And the responsibilities of masters in the South produce for them "more cares and less liberty than the slaves themselves."[15]

Such twisted logic prompted William Lloyd Garrison, editor of the abolitionist newspaper The Liberator, to call George Fitzhugh an "audacious defender of the soul-crushing, blood-reeking system of slavery. He is certainly crack-brained, and deserves pity rather than ridicule or censure."[16]

A mainstay of Fitzhugh's proslavery stand was his biased perception of the concept of equality. He saw inequality, aristocracy, and slavery as the most preferred conditions for living peacefully. "The doctrine of human equality," he bellowed, "is practically impossible, and directly conflicts with... all social existence." He viewed the Declaration of Independence as being in error for stating that all men are created equal. "Men are not born physically, morally, or intellectually equal," a fact which makes the Declaration "false and unmeaning."[17]

Where the achievement of social equality is attempted, people "must from necessity be rivals, antagonists, competitors, and enemies. Self preservation... makes this selfish course of action essential...." The remedy for this self-centered state of affairs was "to identify the interests of the weak and the strong, the poor and the rich. Domestic slavery does this far better than any other institution."

The path to social peace was clear to Fitzhugh. "Subordination, difference of caste and classes, difference of sex, age and slavery beget peace and goodwill." In free society, a laborer usually owns no house, is insecure of employment, and faces the costs of sickness and old age without adequate resources. "In all this," said Fitzhugh, "there is little to incite to virtue, much to tempt to crime, nothing to afford happiness, but quite enough to inflict misery."[18]

According to Fitzhugh, the bane of free society was that "Liberty and equality... [motivate] men in oppressing precisely that part of mankind who most need sympathy, aid and protection." Having said this, he made a statement that contradicted the basic philosophy of the abolitionists: "The bestowing upon men equality of rights is but giving license to the strong to oppress the weak."[19]

Gerrit Smith would remind Fitzhugh that the Declaration of Independence did not "bestow" rights, it only recognized their natural existence, just as no government can either grant or deny human rights. It can only protect naturally equal rights of personhood. Sometimes Fitzhugh did recognize the concept of "universal liberty," as he called it, but did not comprehend its natural origin. He claimed that it "has disintegrated and dissolved society, and placed men in isolated, selfish, and antagonistic positions."

He declared that there is "conclusive proof that liberty and equality have not conduced to enhance the comfort or the happiness of the people." As evidence, he cited trade unions, strikes, crime, and pauperism as symptoms of discontent, and believed that people who like the idea of equality cannot see its faults, and are "reluctant to attribute the evil phenomena which it exhibits to defects inherent in the system itself."[20]

Those defects revolve around the inability of the social institutional system of free society to provide for the needs of its most needy constituents. What Fitzhugh believed to be necessary was a feudal-like structure that he saw clearly operating in slavery-based southern culture. In a classic feudal social system, roles among various strata were founded in obligation.

In Medieval times, a local king divided his land into fiefs ruled by his chosen barons, who in turn divided the fief into manors to be administered by lords. The lords owned everything on their land, including crops and peasants, and provided knights for military service to the king. The lord ruled the lives of 90% of the residents of the manor called peasants, who generally owned nothing, and pledged their labor to their local lord in return for protection.

These relationships among social strata were obligatory, contractual agreements based on reciprocal feudal duties. A pattern of mutual loyalty existed among social levels that assured security for all, sealed with oaths that swore to the consistency of faithful fulfillment of obligations. This is how George Fitzhugh viewed southern slave culture.

He viewed the slave as a grown-up child who behaves in accordance with "impulse, passion, and appetite." Control by law is therefore impossible, so what is needed is a benevolent master to channel the negro's energies into productive labor. Being "improvident," the negro cannot plan for the future, so needs constant supervision. The negro fills the feudal role of peasant with the slave owner or master as his lord. The negro was not stupid or incapable of learning, but needed to be guided into a productive, civilized role by enlightened "lords" who would protect them from oppression in return for their lifetime of service. Their mutual loyalty would benefit both parties: the slave would acquire job stability, dependable supplies of food, clothing, protection and the moralizing influence of Christianity; the "lord and master" would acquire a continuous, predictable supply of cheap labor, and affluence for his family.[21]

According to Fitzhugh, the slaves were the major beneficiaries in this relationship. They receive more benefits for their livelihood than do wage-earners in the North. "Wages are worse than slavery," he claimed, because they provide only part of what a worker needs, thus leading to poverty and sickness. Slavery provides constancy of supply for all needs. Therefore, the slave finds that all his needs are met, and realizes that "his liberty is a curse to himself, and a greater curse to the society around him." Liberty would provide only part of his needs, causing the negro to become a social danger.

"Virginia negroes have become moral and intelligent. They love their master and his family, and the attachment is reciprocated."[22]

> The slave owner, said Fitzhugh, is worse off than the slave because he "is under an obligation legally, theoretically, and practically, to labor [for the slave]. Therefore, the master of... slaves is always a slave himself.... The obligations of the master are more onerous than those of the slave.... [The slave's] situation is less honorable, but far more secure than that of the master."

Fitzhugh conveniently ignored, or perhaps did not realize, the point that the status of "slave" demeans personhood and incites anger. All he saw was that obedience creates order. He noted that the slave's "physical world is but a series of subordinations, and the more perfect the subordination, the greater the harmony and happiness." In a delusional reversal of power, he believed that "The humble and obedient slave exercises more or less control over the most brutal and hard-hearted master." At least he recognized that masters can be brutal.[23]

Believing as he did, Fitzhugh saw the abolitionists' goal of emancipation as ludicrous.

> "A free negro! Why, the very term seems an absurdity.... The Anglo-Saxons of America are the only people in the world fitted for freedom. [In other nations], the emancipation of the blacks has occasioned many evils and been productive of no ostensible good to themselves or to the whites.... It is needless to enumerate the many evils that short-sighted philanthropy has inflicted on... the world... by emancipation."

Fitzhugh angrily railed on, saying:
"neither the feelings nor the interests of any part of the community, except of a few crazy abolitionists, can be enlisted in their behalf.... The free negroes are no doubt an intolerable nuisance. They blight the prosperity of every village and of every country neighborhood where they settle."

Then, in his effort to expand the value of white male dominance, he added,
"We subject children till 21 years of age to the control of their parents.... We subject wives to the dominion of their husbands; apprentices to their masters.... We take away liberties for the good of society.... How cruel and unwise in us not to extend the blessings of slavery to the free negroes."[24]

According to hundreds of slave narratives, they did not see slavery as a blessing, yet Fitzhugh maintained that
"It was a blessing to the negro to be brought from Africa and made a slave and a Christian.... In his proper sphere, we love and respect the negro. He is eminently docile, imitative and parasitical.... Every social structure must have its substratum.... Slavery is natural and necessary, and will in some form insinuate itself into all civilized society."[25]

This insinuation, Fitzhugh believed, is necessary to social order, and requires the elimination of competition and capitalism. If the reformers are sincere in their desire to approach perfectionism—the morally perfect society—then they should embrace slavery because
"No efficient combination of labor can be effected till men give up their liberty of action and subject themselves to a common despotic head or ruler. This is slavery.... Slavery identifies the interests of rich and poor, master and slave, and begets domestic affection on the one side, and loyalty and respect on the other."

Fitzhugh equated the southern slave plantation to an ideal commune. "A southern farm is the beau ideal of Communism." That is, from each according to his means, to each according to his needs. The slave, therefore, has no fear of want, whereas free laborers are always in need. Fitzhugh uses this logic to make "slaves" of free people: "The profits which capital extracts from labor makes free laborers slaves without the rights, privileges, or advantages of domestic slaves; and capitalists their masters with all the advantages, and none of the burdens and obligations of the ordinary owners of slaves."[26]

When they met in Peterboro in the spring of 1855, George Fitzhugh and Gerrit Smith were not enemies. Through their letters over the previous five years, their areas of disagreement had become obvious, yet each was open to listening to, and perhaps educating, the other.

As Fitzhugh put it, "Where, sir, is common ground on which we can meet?" It was available. Neither of them liked slavery. The difference was that Smith saw it as unnecessary, and Fitzhugh thought it was necessary. "Black slavery," said Fitzhugh,

"in its inception and institution is an odious thing, but you and I... agree that God and nature intended a community of property in lands, as well as an air and water—I want to show that this community can only be established through the instrumentality of some form of domestic slavery."

Due to the obligatory relationships prevalent under slavery, he was willing to "cling to it as a humane and proper institution."

Gerrit, of course, saw the opposite.[27]

Whereas Fitzhugh saw freedom in order with low empathy among constituents, Gerrit saw order in freedom with high empathy among constituents. Fitzhugh's tactics were defensive, regressive, and supportive of the status quo; Smith's tactics were offensive, progressive, and supportive of reform. Fitzhugh preferred to rule people with tyrannical methods; Smith preferred to rule lightly with recognition of the value of human diversity. Both wanted a stable human community, with Fitzhugh achieving it through apprenticeship and obligation, and Smith through choice and self-sovereignty. Fitzhugh's ideas died with the Civil War; Smith's legacy was a truly empathic lifestyle clearly implemented throughout his long life. As a sign of intellectual friendship, Smith sent Fitzhugh $20 to support his writing endeavors.

Gerrit Smith was the epitome of reformers. He emerged in the mid-1820s with a new college degree as a representative of an aristocratic family, and a young man rebelling against the self-centeredness of his mercenary father. Having purchased his father's lucrative land sales business, and possessing the philanthropic gene, he was primed for action in humane works.

Having languished in the ideational doldrums for about four decades since the founding of the new United States, the smoldering issue of slavery was about to erupt. Gerrit had studied the progressive, liberal philosophers at Hamilton College, and saw direct application of such ideas to the emancipation of slaves. When he entered the antislavery crusade in the mid-1830s, he soon developed a reputation for taking radical stands. His sometimes zealous and extreme statements in speeches and writings earned him the title of a crazy fanatic.

Such was the lot of many reformers. They disregarded public approval and popularity in favor of what their conscience told them was right. They often felt and acted alone without expectation of quick success. Their effort was to make noise about a particular issue, create public awareness, and perhaps recruit interested people into the growing movement.

The risks taken by reformers were not new in the history of the nation. A few decades earlier, the revolutionaries risked their lives and honor for the cause of liberty, and were seen as heroes and respected leaders. But when this same motive inspired reform-minded people to take risks for oppressed people, they were seen as irrational, misguided fools. This difference in perception exposed the entrenched racism in American culture that inhibited progress toward liberty and justice for all.

Although this built-in headwind frustrated the reformers, it did not deter them. As Gerrit Smith acknowledged, "I am accustomed to express my convictions at whatever expense to my reputation."[28]

The mental foundation for such thought in Gerrit Smith was his unusual ability to subvert the accepted tendency to think in terms of dichotomies. The generally accepted pattern of thought was to view concepts and people in terms of contrasting opposites. For instance, water is either hot or cold; an idea is either good or bad; people are either black or white. This is sometimes called dualistic thinking—seeing two qualities that emphasize separation and difference, rather than one unifying quality. In the case of humans, seeing white persons or black persons emphasizes differences, encourages thoughts of superiority or inferiority, and obscures the similarities inherent in personhood.

Gerrit Smith emphasized personhood as the primary human quality, thereby breaking down the stigmatizing dichotomy of black/white. The proper way to view such a concept as color, Smith maintained, was on a continuum that ranged from pure black on one end to pure white on the other end. All examples in between the two extremes were, of course, mixed. Any single example was always a combination of both black and white, so they were never separated as opposites. This is how he viewed people, so claiming that someone was "black" or "white" was unfair. Everyone is a combination of both.

Another aspect of Smith's thought that encouraged empathy was what he called the "head versus heart" issue. If one's habit was to think with the head, emphasis would be placed on logic, reason, law, and authority. This type of thinking leads to an acceptance of the status quo. Thinking with the heart places emphasis on emotions and feelings, leading to empathy and challenging the status quo. All thinking is complex enough to involve both head and heart, but Gerrit's point was that feelings ought to be important enough to produce facts, thereby inspiring empathy. Thinking with—or from—the heart enables one to share features of human existence by feeling what other people feel to the point of being able to commit oneself to the pursuit of a better life for others. Thus, Gerrit's commitment to reform, even to the point of developing a "black heart" that felt no superiority of race.[29]

The relevance of these thought processes to the theme herein is that Gerrit's thought was grounded in a heart full of passionate emotions that drove empathy and led to reform; George Fitzhugh's thinking was grounded in a head full of logic and reason that led to personal desire for superiority. The feelings involved in heart-thought can become intense when one senses the pain of discrimination, thereby leading to unconventional and radical solutions to aid the oppressed.

Gerrit's public stands affirming the biological and social equality of black and white people enraged many head-thinkers to the point of committing violence. In the late 1830s, mobs of proslavery thinkers attacked abolitionists like Smith for daring to claim that constitutional protection of free speech allowed them to promulgate such ideas. Perhaps, because of the social volatility of the slavery issue, Smith's public speech went beyond that protection—like shouting "fire" in a crowded theater.

One result of this radical nature of the speech and actions of abolitionists was that it made the 1860 moderate opinions of Abraham Lincoln appear to be conservative enough to lead to his election to the presidency, thereby promoting the process of emancipation of slaves. It even makes sense to think that without the loud, frequent, and radical expression of abolition goals by abolitionists—especially those from New York like Smith, Frederick Douglass, John Brown, Henry B. Stanton, and Elizabeth Cady Stanton—there might not have been a Civil War. Their rhetoric angered southern proslavery people to the degree that they eventually shot at northerners, thereby starting a war.

Gerrit was fond of saying that he liked slavery because opinions about it clearly revealed the character of others. If they supported it, he saw moral weakness in the care-less attitude concerning the quality of life faced by oppressed people who were at the mercy of someone else's power. To those who believed that slavery was legal in either state or federal law, he pointed out that any human law that contradicts the Natural Law of innate equality is void. He believed that every adult person knew the Golden Rule, and could therefore feel the pain of slavery. Claiming otherwise ignored reality and demeaned humanity by tolerating slavery like the family's closeted secret. No institution, he felt, could be more ironic or out of place amid the revolutionary spirit of freedom upon which the country was founded.

In his speech before Congress as a United States Congressman in April of 1854, Gerrit based his argument against the legality of slavery on the Declaration of Independence. It stated that "all men [people?] are created equal," and possess "unalienable rights." Because this document preceded the writing of the United States Constitution, it affirms the fact that slavery has always been illegal in this country. The legal status of the Declaration notwithstanding, Gerrit's point is clear—in a moral sense, slavery is not acceptable as a proper relationship among people. Human beings cannot own other human beings. One's natural, innate right to freedom he refers to as the "great center truth" of our country. Gerrit's main point of opposition to slavery was not the abuse of the slave, but the idea that one human can own another. As he put it:

"Were all the whips and instruments of human torture at the South burnt up, and were there no lack of assurance that all the slaves of the South would, in all future time, be well fed and well clothed, the abolitionists would see no reason for abating... their righteous warfare against the doctrine that immortal, God-redeemed man may be the property of his fellow man."[30]

And in his Congressional speech against slavery:
"Slavery is a conspiracy... of the strong against the weak.... Who ever heard of a law to uphold a conspiracy?... The law of human equality was written by the finger of God on the heart of man, [but]... while men despise fraud, and loathe rapine, and abhor

blood, they will reject with indignation the wild and guilty fantasy that man can hold property in man."[31]

Gerrit knew that if slavery were legal, either the laws of nature or the laws of man were wrong, and in accordance with his liberal philosophy, natural law could not be wrong. As antislavery Brit James Ramsey had written, "Had nature intended negroes for slavery, they would've been born without any sentiment for liberty."[32]

In order to make a point vividly clear, Smith was expert at using analogies. He once likened the institution of slavery to a wolf devouring sheep. Would the farmer compromise with the wolf or kill it? "And the people of the North, in letting slavery live, and in making bargains with it, act no less absurdly than would the farmer who would... share with the wolf."[33]

> Trying to show how debasing slavery is, Gerrit wrote a Virginia slave owner: "in the free states, we refuse to the colored man the right of suffrage, the right of a respectable seat in our churches, our private houses, our [railroad] cars and steamboats.... We studiously close upon him the avenues to respectability and happiness; and, in short, we tax our ingenuity to make him feel that he is an outcast from society, and that his appropriate place is in the deepest debasement.... [Yet], sure I am, that the case is not yet to be known, where a free person of color in one of the free States sighs for a return to the prison house of slavery."[34]

As this quote shows, Smith knew that the extent of racial discrimination in the North was widespread and intense, and contaminated support of our fundamental notions of freedom and equality. It baffled him that people could not see the derogatory effect of prejudice on democracy, and he asked,

> "Shall we never cease from this prejudice? Born and bred, as I was, among negroes and Indians as well as whites, and respecting and loving all equally well, this insane prejudice is well-nigh incomprehensible to me."

He viewed it as being reinforced by selfishness that could be overcome by allowing one's conscience to rule. Optimistically, Smith believed that every human in his naturally conceived conscience was an abolitionist. "The slaveholder himself is an abolitionist" because he inherently understands "the preciousness of personal liberty." "The slaveholders," Smith said, "never testify so strongly against slavery, as when they tell us that their slaves are light-hearted and happy."

This happens, he said, because slaveholders project onto the slave what they hope would be true. But they are just delusional, and deserve to be pitied.[35]

Given Gerrit Smith's liberal ideas and commitment to reform, what could he do about slavery? The major and powerful social institutions at the beginning of the reform era supported slavery. All Christian denominations supported it to some degree; the two major political parties—Democrat and Whig—supported it; businesses favored slavery because of investments in its products. Where could one start to work against such entrenched power?

There were no precedents in former successful social movements of reform to learn from. There were no proven techniques of producing social change. There were no major supportive institutions to provide personnel, funding or networks of communication and influence. There were no formal organizations to join and work for antislavery goals. The nascent abolitionists had to create new ways of battling against intimidating foes. Certain that their moral stand for equality was correct, they even had to work in opposition to hypocritical governments. "That we are a nation for liberty is among our wildest conceits," said Smith. "American slavery has brought disgrace upon the principles [of equality and justice]."[36]

Without any precedents or cultural background for producing fundamental changes in the established social fabric, how did young people schooled in liberal social philosophy get started in building an abolition movement?

Because women were not allowed to participate in public, political activity in the early 1830s, it was men who ignited the abolition fuse. Many of them faced a critical moment—a turning point—that catapulted them into action. For William Lloyd Garrison, it was being jailed in Baltimore for having publicly condemned a slave owner. For John Brown, it was watching a slave being beaten. For Wendell Phillips, it was the murder of antislavery journalist Elijah Lovejoy. For Gerrit Smith, it was a mob of high-class citizens in Utica that prevented free speech.

Before the advent of "immediatism" in the early 1830s, those interested in antislavery work were attracted to the American Colonization Society. Founded in January of 1817 by Virginia Congressman Charles Fenton Mercer, the ACS intended to send free blacks back to Africa in order to cleanse the United States of their pernicious influence. Many future abolitionists started here, but soon saw its racist goals and opted out. When William Lloyd Garrison published his first edition of The Liberator, an antislavery newspaper, in Boston on January 1, 1831, he set the stage for the social movement that would eventually put an end to slavery. His main idea was to make interracial prejudice the focus of a social war. Gerrit called slavery "a state of war," and was lured into the new movement.

The tactics approved of by the Boston-based leadership of this early stage of the movement were called "moral suasion"—a form of preaching to slaveowners to voluntarily move away from the sin of owning people. Gerrit had joined a Christian church in 1826, and found this approach initially appealing. Ann was in full agreement, having been the main influence on Gerrit's conversion. In the 1830s, she became actively involved with him in his travels.

The non-violent emphasis and vocal activity of the moral suasion technique was a secular-based evangelical effort to convince slaveowners of their immorality. It is not surprising that it did not work well. Slave owners were less interested in truth based on natural law than they were in profits from slave labor. The optimism of these early abolitionists that racism could be defeated by righteous thoughts exposes their naïveté. As Garrison put it, "It did not occur to us that nearly every religious sect and every political party would side with the oppressor." The result was that by 1839, practical thinkers like Gerrit Smith were disillusioned, and looking for other tactics that would be more effective.

Gerrit Smith was a practical dreamer. That intentional oxymoron expresses what his critics saw as inconsistencies in his thought and action. His approach to problems was practical: if the tool being used to accomplish a goal is not working, choose a better tool. For instance, rather than continue trying to dig a big hole with a trowel, get a shovel. Hence, when it became obvious that moral suasion was not producing the desired results, Smith and three of his abolitionist colleagues met in the Smith house in 1839 in Peterboro to discuss the possibility of forming a third political party to pursue the abolition of slavery. Both major parties were proslavery.

This switch in Smith's antislavery tactics illustrates his practical approach to problems. Moral suasion was a theoretical solution, politics a practical one. And he made more switches in tactics later. Historian Aileen Kraditor astutely commented that Gerrit Smith's opinions and tactics regarding abolition "constitute a good weather vane showing the direction of the ideological wind in the abolitionist movement."[37]

Gerrit's adoption of political tactics is a curiosity, and makes sense only in light of his practicality. No one in the Smith family was oriented in favor of political activity personally. They all avoided it. Gerrit turned to politics with serious doubts because he knew that a moral-based attitude change in the general public was necessary before racial discrimination could be conquered. The only way political activity could succeed in abolishing slavery was by means of the legal process of passing laws to prohibit it. If that were to occur, slavery would be illegal, thereby changing the rules of the social game, but not the score. The intent to discriminate would continue.

Adding to the curiosity is the fact that Gerrit did not like politicians because they generally placed a higher priority on being elected than on principled, moral goals. Also, he had no desire to become a politician himself. He claimed to be poorly read, and unaware of the skills necessary to be a statesman. "It will be long," he said, "before I consent to be, and very long, before I ask to be a candidate for civil office...."[38]

In spite of Smith's attitude about participating in politics, his constituents nominated him for president of the United States four times, for governor of New York State three times, and for the United States Congress once. He had pleaded with the public not to nominate him, and, when nominated, refused to campaign, and asked constituents not to vote for him. But in the fall of 1852, he was elected to Congress as an independent from his district that was composed mainly of Madison and Oswego Counties.

Although his family was not thrilled about his departure for Washington, D.C., many abolitionists were. Finally, they sighed, there would be a respected voice for abolition in Congress. During his tenure there, he made several brilliant speeches on the floor of the House of Representatives in support of abolition, but had very little influence on the direction of national policy.

The national government at that time was dominated by slaveowners in all its branches. Journalists referred to "The Slave Power" as controlling the direction of national social policy. The result for Gerrit was frustration. No one was listening to his moral message. He concluded that his antislavery effort would achieve more success through his work in Peterboro, so after serving only one-half of his two-year term, he resigned and returned home.

The most effective political move made by Gerrit was a successful establishment of the Liberty Party as an alternative to the Democrat and Whig parties. Following the initial 1839 meeting in the Smith house, a series of conventions was held around Upstate New York to gather support for the new party. During the 1840s, the Liberty Party fielded candidates at all governmental levels, achieving some success at local levels, especially in the township of Smithfield where Gerrit lived.

The Abolition of Slavery

At the national level, the first Liberty Party presidential candidate in 1840 was James Gillespie Birney. Throughout the 1840s, the party grew in its vote-gathering ability as it spread the message for abolishing slavery. In 1854, it coalesced with other antislavery factions to form the Republican Party. Abraham Lincoln became the 1860 Republican Party presidential candidate, and went on to write the Emancipation Proclamation in 1863, and helped to ratify the thirteenth amendment to the United States Constitution in 1865, thereby legally abolishing slavery.

A very significant point that derives from this brief coverage of Gerrit Smith's relation to politics involves the 1839 meeting of Gerrit and his colleagues—Utica lawyer Alvan Stuart, journalist James Gillespie Birney, and politician and former Erie Canal Commissioner Myron Holley. This meeting around the hearth in Gerrit's living room, with the full support of his family, was the initial step in a fifteen-year process that led to the formation of the Republican Party—the party that still exists today.

When formed in 1854, the Republican Party was the party of ultra-liberal, radical human rights activists in pursuit of the abolition of slavery. This new party reflected well the ethos of the Smith family—love everybody. Every person was perceived as having value, even slaveowners. As Gerrit put it, "All sound statesmanship is warmed and vitalized by love, and... the statesmanship of which love is not the soul is exceedingly pernicious as well as utterly spurious." By the end of the nineteenth century, that philosophical orientation of the Republican Party had changed to conservatism. That party looks much different today than it did in Gerrit's day.[39]

A corollary development to the work of the Liberty Party was the founding of the "Free Church" as part of the Union Church Movement in the 1840s. The idea was to unify antislavery Christians in organizations outside of the proslavery Christian denominations. In 1843, the Smith family led a local effort in Peterboro to escape from the proslavery local Presbyterian Church, and establish a Free Church of Peterboro that would have no denominational affiliation, and be open to any Christian worshipers. It met for four years in the Temperance Hotel on the Smith property before building its own meetinghouse on the southeastern corner of the Peterboro green.

The significant point of this Smith family effort was the influence of the Free Church within the antislavery movement. The church actually became a surrogate antislavery society. It organized antislavery events, supported antislavery political candidates, and invited antislavery speakers to its podium. This orientation angered many supporters of slavery, especially because it melded the supposedly separate spheres of religion and politics. As such, it became a powerful tool in the antislavery arsenal. The Free Church actually undertook some of the functions of the American Anti-slavery Society after it lost much of its power due to a split in the movement in 1840.

Another significant aspect of the abolition movement that required the agreement and total cooperation among all the members of the Gerrit and Ann Smith family was their successful operation of a major station on the underground railroad. This process obligated a family—indeed, a community—to such a high level of dedication to the cause of freedom for former slaves that they were willing to take extreme risks. Their commitment to achieving freedom for others was founded in their sense of morality.

The underground railroad conveyed a moral message; it was a moral statement about a corrupt nation whose goals of justice and freedom for all were intentionally unmet. As such, the symbolic value of the underground railroad became legendary, and its success or failure represented trends within the abolition movement as a whole. If freedom for the slaves was not achieved, the Smiths thought, then the life of the new nation was in jeopardy. Denial of freedom is a formula for revolution, and even as early as 1845, Gerrit could see the coming of a violent war that would end slavery and perhaps destroy the nation. As his friend James G. Birney wrote in a letter to Gerrit:

"The antagonistic principles of liberty and slavery have been roused into action and one or the other must be victorious.

There will be no cessation of the strife, until slavery shall be exterminated, or liberty destroyed."[40]

The Smiths viewed their work for the underground railroad as a practical expression of their piety. "For many years," wrote Gerrit to William Seward, "I have regarded the helping of slaves to liberty, especially at the great peril of the helper, as among the most beautiful expressions and among the most decisive evidences of disinterested benevolence and genuine piety."[41]

Gerrit liked to see quickly visible and tangible results of his philanthropy, and the work for fugitive slaves offered that. He would see first-hand the horrifying experiences that former slaves had endured, and that touched his heart. In an 1838 letter to the editor of the Union Herald, Gerrit wrote:

"My dear Sir:— You will be happy to hear, that the two fugitive slaves, to whom in the brotherly love of your heart, you gave the use of your horse, are still making undisturbed progress towards the *monarchical* land whither *republican* slaves escape for the enjoyment of liberty. They had eaten their breakfast, and were seated in my wagon, before day-dawn, this morning.

Fugitive slaves have before taken my house in their way, but never any, whose lips and persons made so forcible an appeal to my sensibilities, and kindled in me so much abhorrence of the hell-concocted system of American slavery.

The fugitives exhibited their bare backs to myself and a number of my neighbors. Williams' back is comparatively scarred. But, I speak within bounds, when I say, that one-third to one-half of the whole surface of the back and shoulders of poor Scott, *consists of scars and wales resulting from innumerable gashes*. His natural complexion being yellow and the callous places being nearly black, his back and shoulders remind you of a spotted animal."[42]

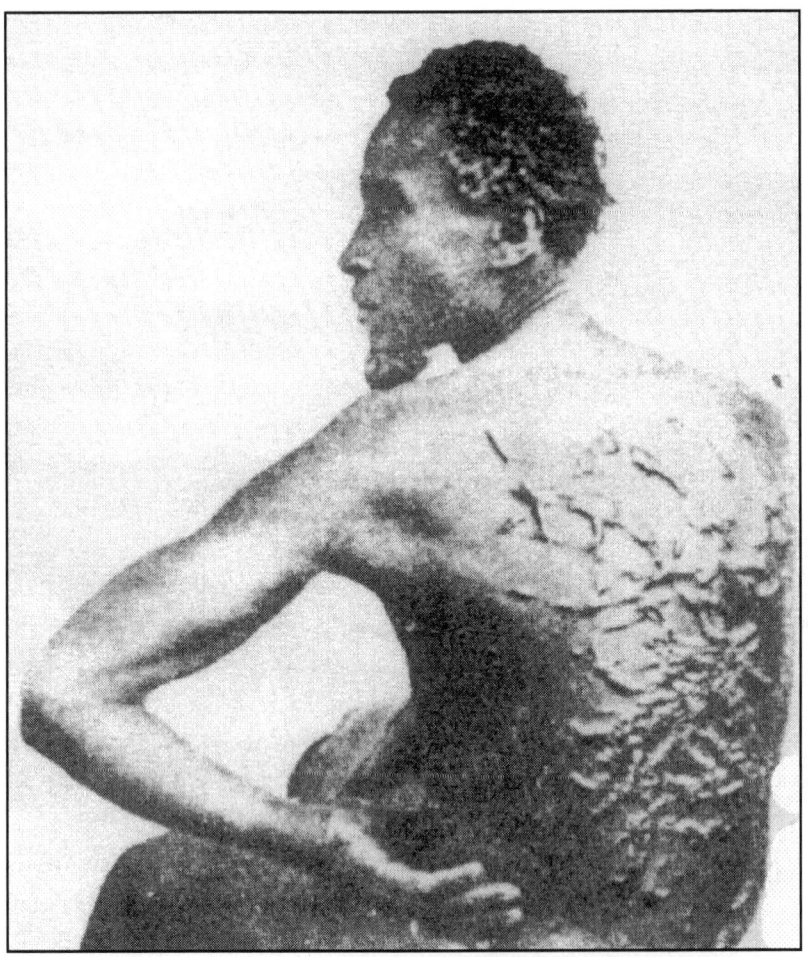

This photograph of a slave's back, almost completely coered by scars from whippings, was an example of proof of creulty and torture that served as evidence for the opponents of slavery.

From the author's collection

There were many young, black men similar to these that received aid from the Smith family in Peterboro, perhaps as many as one thousand. Gerrit identified with their plight so completely that, at times, he called himself "a colored man," and the family gave freely of its resources to them in the form of clothing, food, money, transportation, and, most importantly, their perception of the runaway as a dignified and respected person.

The Smiths' Peterboro underground railroad station was a preferred stop on the northward route, and was highly recommended by stations south of Peterboro. There was no map of routes headed north for runaways to follow, and no previous knowledge on their part of where to go. Once on their way north, they relied on word-of-mouth for directions, perhaps going to Peterboro because that is where someone directed them.

One "conductor" who traveled the underground railroad route north while bringing other runaways with her was Harriet Tubman. She liked to go through Peterboro—perhaps several times—because she knew that as the last stop en route to Canada, the rest of the trip was a cinch thanks to the plentiful resources available through the Smith family. Harriet knew all four members of the Smith family, each of whom helped her in some way.

Gerrit's connection to Canada was through his Oswego business agent John B. Edwards. Gerrit owned wharf property along the east bank of the Oswego Canal that required constant attention for renters. Edwards, also an abolitionist, filled that role. He was hired in 1831, and worked peacefully and cooperatively with Gerrit for forty-three years. After Gerrit died in 1874, Edwards stayed on in Oswego to manage the continuing business there. His role relative to the underground railroad appears clearly in the letters written between him and Gerrit. Edwards wrote on average every other day, informing Gerrit on business matters relating to the Oswego property. Within the business-related information in his three-to-five-page letters are "asides"—words supposed to be for Gerrit's eyes only—that refer to his actions on behalf of former slaves headed for Canada. An example:
"The Fugitive Slave Dorsey came to me today with your letter. I have just put him aboard a vessel bound for Canada, and gave him $1.00." Edwards had connections with sympathetic ship captains who would accept runaway slaves.

One way that Ann and Elizabeth participated helpfully in the underground railroad occurred when there was obvious risk for the runaway in Peterboro. They helped to disguise the former slave by dressing him in feminine clothing in order to avoid capture during the trip from Peterboro to Oswego.

Another example of the Smith family's commitment to abolition and freedom for slaves is evident in their support for the purchase of slaves. Gerrit was sometimes criticized for being a slave dealer. He did buy slaves, but it was for the purpose of setting them free. This was another way that Gerrit could see and feel the quick results of his philanthropy. He spoke of

> "the great delight I take in purchasing the Liberty of slaves.... None of my expenditures of money have brought me more gladness of heart."[44]

The best example of this that involved the whole Smith family occurred in 1841. Having been born into a slave-owning family in Maryland, Ann was reared in part by a slave "nanny," a nursemaid named Harriet Sims. When Ann's family sold their slaves and moved to Upstate New York in 1817, Harriet Sims was given to Ann's older brother James Fitzhugh as a slave. Harriet eventually married another Fitzhugh slave named Samuel Russell with whom she had several children.

When Ann's father, William Fitzhugh, died in 1839, Ann remembered her former nursemaid. She felt guilty about Harriet's status as a slave, and she asked if Gerrit, with his newly developed abolitionist perspective, would find Harriet and purchase her freedom. James Fitzhugh had sold Harriet and Samuel Russell, who were eventually located as the property of slaveowner Samuel Worthington in Mississippi. Smith sent an agent, James C. Fuller (an abolitionist from Skaneateles, New York) to Kentucky, where the Worthingtons were spending the summer, to transact the business of purchase.

The two parties agreed on the price of $3,500. The letter sent by the Smiths to the Russells informing them of their freedom is quoted in full:

> "Dear friends, We have purchased your liberty and that of your five children, and paid therefor $3500. In addition, we have paid

several hundred dollars to defray your travelling expenses and those of the dear friend James C. Fuller who went for you. We now consent to let you occupy until 1st April next without rent the small white house opposite Mr. Scofield's. The few articles of clothing which we let you have and of furniture which consist of beds, bedding, table, chairs, etc. etc.—we give you. We also give you ten dollars in money. And now we say to you that this little outfit is all in the way of property, which you are to expect from us. For the means of your subsistence hereafter you are to look under God to your own industry + frugality + prudence. Our advice is, that Samuel should seek employment immediately in one of the large towns in this vicinity—and that the two oldest girls be put into families where they will be fed + clothed + educated without any expense to yourselves. We beg you to be very industrious—and to lay up as much as you can of your earnings, so that you may in the course of four or five years be able to buy a little home for yourselves. But above all, we beg you to seek the salvation of your own and your childrens' souls, and to lay up treasure in Heaven.

Your friends,
Gerrit Smith
Ann C. Smith [45]

The youngest of the five Russell children who came to freedom in Peterboro was Malvina. She lived in Peterboro and worked for the Smith family until her death in 1925.

The last chronological stage of the Smith family's commitment to the abolition movement revolves around John Brown and his advocacy of violence as the proper tactic to use in defeating slavery. On February 23, 1858, abolitionist John Brown was in Peterboro for his fifth visit with the Gerrit Smith family. Also visiting was Franklin Benjamin Sanborn, a young educator from Boston who was one of a group of six—"The Secret Six"—who were financial supporters of Brown's

Malvina Russell was the daughter of Ann Smith's childhood nursemaid, Harriet Sims. The Smiths bought her family's freedom from a Mississippi slave owner in 1841, and Malvina lived in Peterboro until her death in 1925, working many years for the Smith family.

From the author's collection

clandestine activities to subvert slavery. Brown was in Peterboro to ask the group of six for a final infusion of funds before he carried out his plan to invade Harpers Ferry, Virginia in an effort to encourage slaves to seek freedom.

Sanborn was the only member of the five supporters from the Boston area to be present in Peterboro at Gerrit's invitation. The winter weather in February had deterred the others from travel. Sanborn and Smith walked in the snow-covered meadow behind the house to discuss the funding of Brown's potentially treasonous plan, while Brown waited inside for their answer. Smith felt compelled to fund the violence, even though he was the vice president of the American Peace Society.

As a supporter of non-violence, it seems odd that Gerrit Smith would sanction violent action as a proper tactic for ending slavery, but by the late 1850s, he was becoming burned-out, having spent over two decades struggling to achieve the abolition of slavery with no success. Perhaps, he thought, the plan of this radical John Brown might work. And what was there to lose? Violence between the North and the South was looming in the near future. The tragedy of this decision to fund Brown was both personal and national.

At the national level, Brown's invasion of Harpers Ferry did eventually trigger a civil war. The war probably would have happened even without Brown's actions, and it may have been, as Brown maintained, a necessary step in ending slavery.

At the personal level, three weeks after the October 16, 1859 attack at Harpers Ferry, Gerrit Smith had what today might be called a 'nervous breakdown' and was admitted to the Utica Asylum for the Insane under the care of the progressive "psychiatrist" John P. Gray. Smith was treated for a bipolar, manic-depressive syndrome, and spent only four weeks at the hospital. His psychotic episode was actually the result of a decade-long struggle to adjust to increasing levels of stress produced by a variety of serious burdens.

During the decade of the 1850s, the Smith family dealt with a series of stressful conditions. Even as a young boy, Greene was a rebel.

In the late 1850s as a teenager, he defied his family's attempts to mold him into a Christian and a businessman. He was a major source of friction between Ann and Gerrit. Ann wished to let him become what he wanted to be, while Gerrit badgered him to conform to his father's demands.

Also in the mid-1850s, Ann and Gerrit faced a 'mid-life crisis'. Gerrit was distressed over the tears caused by their relationship, and wondered if he should have kept his "single bed." Ann wept over the waning of their love, saying that "the future makes me sad." They did weather this storm, but the stress it produced added to that coming from their disagreements about Greene.

Gerrit's physical health was also a big concern in the 1850s. He battled typhoid fever which nearly killed him, and he had a chronic problem with the pain of hemorrhoids. Three operations failed to cure the hemorrhoids, and caused long periods of convalescence.

Also in the 1850s, the family dealt with public ridicule concerning the new brand of religion that Gerrit had invented—the "Religion of Reason." Critics accused them of blasphemy, irreverence, and hypocrisy, and questioned their loyalty to Christian principles.

When the burdens of these sources of stress were compounded by the capture and trial of John Brown, Gerrit worried about being arrested for treason against the United States, temporarily lost contact with reality, and needed some short-term therapy to help him become stable again.

The trauma of Gerrit's brief psychological illness illustrates well the trials endured by the Smith family as they steered through the winding currents of social reform. They supported one another through ordeals that might have overwhelmed an individual, and together steadied their unstable ship of reform.

To summarize this unit on the Smith family's participation in the movement to abolish slavery, it is wise to review the reasons why their anger was piqued, their dedication was high, and their passion was intense.

As well-educated, liberal thinkers, they viewed prejudice about anyone as evil. In the post-revolutionary period into which they were born, the clear contradiction between democracy and tyranny, freedom and bondage, good and evil, permeated every aspect of life throughout the country. Friction among people and ideas—even to the point of conflict—was everywhere. There were arguments in the home, in churches, in legislatures, in village stores, in political gatherings, and, eventually, on the battlefield. The weapons used ranged from ideas and words, to whips, chains, and bullets. Every aspect of one's life—moral, economic, social, political, philosophical, and personal—was influenced by the issue of slavery.

Slavery was not just an institution in the South. Its supporters and critics were everywhere, and their positions were so rigid that mutual understanding and compromise was impossible. To southerners, all northerners were John Browns; to northerners, all southerners were Simon LeGrees. In the end, it was the moral issue of stolen freedom that won the battle, while the practical issues of business profit and subordination were subdued. But before the Civil War when the opposing ideas clashed, intense emotions and burning passions made enemies of neighbors.

The Smiths sided with freedom, and they were tuned in to the statements of the critics of American culture. Quoting a few of those critical statements will help to explain the origin of the Smiths' passion.

Timothy Dwight, a Connecticut pastor and future president of Yale University, stated his concerns poetically:
"O thou chief curse, since curses here began;
First guilt, first woe, first infamy of man;
Thou spot of hell, deep smirch'd on human kind,
The uncur'd gangrene of the reasoning mind;
Alike in church, in state, and household all,
Supreme memorial of the world's dread fall;
O Slavery! laurel of the Infernal mind,
Proud Satan's triumph over lost mankind!"[46]

The London Evangelical Magazine bellowed:
"The United States of America present to the world one of the most extraordinary spectacles that can be conceived by the mind of man. They are a huge moral and political enigma. We behold part of the population priding themselves on the peculiar freedom of their institutions, and holding the other part in the shackles of slavery.... The national emblem of the American states... the eagle, with liberty on his wings, should... clutch in his talons the manacled and writhing form of the colored man."

Edward Strutt Abdy, an English legal academic and abolitionist, wrote that American slavery is
"a mockery and disgrace of the American character,... a Christian people excelling all the heathen tribes of the world in systematic wickedness, a free republic exercising greater oppression than was ever heard of in the old king-scourged and priest-ridden despotisms of Europe."

And from the Edinburgh Review, a Scottish journal:
"Every American who loves his country should dedicate his whole life, and every faculty of his soul, to efface the foul blot of slavery from its character."[47]

In the United States, the critics shouted. African-American abolitionist William Wells Brown wrote to Boston abolitionist Wendell Phillips:
"We may search history in vain to find a people who have sunk themselves as low, and made themselves appear as infamous by their treatment of their fellow men, as have the people of the United States.... In most of the states we are disfranchised, our children are shut out from the public schools, and embarrassments are thrown in the way of every attempt to elevate ourselves. And after they have degraded us, sold us, mobbed us, and done everything in their power to oppress us, then, if we wish to leave the country, they refuse us passports

upon the grounds that we are not citizens.... [They are sinking] lower and lower in the estimation of the good and wise of all lands."[48]

When the Synod of Illinois withdrew from the Lutheran General Assembly over the slavery issue in 1849, it stated that
"slavery is wickedness framed by law; and as a system, is made up of such unnatural and monstrous enactments as are expressly and knowingly formed, fitted and intended to crush millions of our fellow-men down into mere chattels or property, to be bought and sold like brutes—stripping them of their rights, as rational, voluntary, accountable beings; tearing God's image out of them; sundering their most sacred obligations and relations; trampling underfoot their dearest and most tender ties, and making them the doomed victims of avarice, caprice, cruelty, lust, degradation, and moral ruin."[49]

Even our founding father Thomas Jefferson stated as early as 1785, "What an incomprehensible machine is man! Who can... inflict on his fellow man a bondage, one hour of which is fraught with more misery than ages of that which he rose in rebellion to oppose."[50]

As the Smiths read these kinds of pronouncements, it is no wonder that their emotions triggered a "heart" reaction that fueled their fiery passion for pursuing natural human rights for all persons. And their frequent meetings with abolitionist colleagues at their Peterboro mansion "retreat" reinforced their attitudes and commitment. Their friend and visitor Angelina Grimké wrote,
"I would gladly bury in oblivion all recollection of those scenes [from my childhood in a slave-owning family];... but this cannot be. They come over my memory like gory spectres, and [I must] in the name of humanity; for the sake of the slave holder, as well as the slave, bear witness to the horrors of the southern prison house."

She and her husband Theodore Dwight Weld compiled in 1839 hundreds of slave narratives of their experiences in a book that the Smiths certainly owned—"American Slavery as it Is."

These testimonies to the brutality of slavery helped to initiate a grassroots anti-slavery movement, and generate disgust and dedication among people determined to do something about it. Interestingly, the movement found its most fertile ground in rural areas where small family businesses and farming dominated the economic scene. Capitalist urban interests were less attracted to abolition due to connections with southern states. The networks of support for abolition that grew in the northern states developed links among interested people that spread the news and the passion.

The Smiths aided this process by helping to establish local anti-slavery organizations, free church units in Central New York communities, and the funding of antislavery literature and activities. They funded Frederick Douglass' effective and far-reaching journalistic work, Harriet Tubman's work on the underground railroad, John Brown's plan to agitate for emancipation on southern soil, and the Liberty Party effort to mobilize voters against slavery.

Their efforts to help build an antislavery movement were seriously inhibited by the lack of subscription to that goal by the major social institutions of the time. Religious, political, and economic leaders would generally not commit to abolition as a worthy goal, so abolitionists like the Smiths were on their own to experiment and devise a plan to build enough power to accomplish the abolition of slavery. As their colleague John Rankin put it early in the movement,

"Let all the friends of justice and suffering humanity do what they can, in their several circles, and according to their various stations, capacities and opportunities, and all their little streams of exertion will, in process of time, flow together, and constitute a mighty river that shall sweep away the yoke of oppression, and purge our nation from the abominations of slavery."[52]

A fascinating aspect of the Smith family's antislavery work was their commitment to liberating not just the slave, but also liberating the slaveowner from the suffocating and stagnating grip of prejudice. In a spirit of reconciliation, Gerrit forgave the debts of southern clients after the Civil War, and he traveled to Richmond, Virginia to contribute $25,000 to former Confederate President Jefferson Davis' bail bond and sign for his release from prison.[53]

As a final note of interest, after the Civil War was won by the North, and the thirteenth amendment abolished slavery, its apologist George Fitzhugh capitulated to the antislavery arguments that he had formerly railed against. Obviously, he could no longer apologize for an institution that had died. He became conciliatory, saying,

> "Love is a pleasanter passion than hate, and we have been hating so intensely for the last six years, that we are now looking about for something to love.... We are resolved to hate no one, and to quarrel with no one."

Ann and Gerrit Smith most certainly agreed.

~ 4 ~

Women's Rights

If we believed that equal rights among all persons existed, there would be no need to call attention to "gay rights," or "African-American rights," or "women's rights." These categories of thought exist because we know that equity in treatment of all persons is still a dream. Most importantly, we should note that there is no need to speak about "white male rights," and there is no social movement to pursue equity of treatment for them. Why is that not necessary? Because they hold social power over all the other categories.

We celebrate Black History Month and Women's History Month, but not White Male History Month because every month is dominated by them. The history of the United States has traditionally been written as "his-story" instead of "her-story" or "their story." As previously noted, researching women in this country is made difficult by the fact that her papers and accomplishments are often shrouded under the weight of the assumed importance of males. As British philosopher Herbert Spencer put it, "Our laws are based on the sufficiency of man's rights, and society exists today for women only in so far as she is in the keeping of some man." Women have not held positions of importance outside of the household in the estimation of most historians. Elizabeth Cady Stanton has attracted attention to the biblical fact that woman was an "afterthought" in the story of creation, having been made from the rib of a man.[1]

Cady Stanton viewed Christianity as a major force maintaining the subservience of women. Gerrit Smith agreed with her on this

Elizabeth Cady at age 20. She was Gerrit Smith's cousin, and she spent many days at his Peterboro home.
From the Brigham Young University Photoarchives

---

point, calling the Bible a pernicious book written by males who were attempting to secure power for themselves. Stanton saw Christian leaders as doing all in their power to make a woman's "bondage... more certain and lasting, her degradation more helpless and complete." She asked, "Is the bondage of the priest-ridden [woman] less galling than that of the slave because we do not see the chains, the indelible scars, the festering wounds, the deep degradation...?" Women, she said, felt all these effects just as does the slave.[2]

Elizabeth Cady Stanton's significance in this coverage of the Smith family's influence during the reform era may seem peripheral, but it is not. She was not only a first cousin to the Smiths. As a teenager, she

lived with "cousin Gerrit" and Ann in Peterboro for months at a time during summers, and referred to those days as
> "memorable [and] among the most charming in my life.... I felt a new inspiration in life and was enthused with new ideas of individual rights..., for the anti-slavery platform was the best school the American people ever had on which to learn republican principles and ethics.... The discussions at my cousin's fireside I count among the great blessings of my life."[3]

The people that the young Elizabeth Cady met at the Smiths' hearth molded the rest of her life. Visitors included aristocratic members of old Dutch families like the Van Rensselaers, the Schuylers, and the Livingstons; abolitionists like Beriah Green and Henry Brewster Stanton; and, most importantly, Native Americans of the Oneida Nation.

From their business relationship with Peter Smith in the late 1700s to their continuing friendly relationship with Gerrit and Ann Smith in the 1830s, Native Americans were frequently present in Peterboro. Through her direct contact with them, Elizabeth learned about the social structure of their culture. Matriarchy was the pattern of rule that directed their lives and structure of their government.

In a matriarchy, women hold the political and economic power, making all decisions relating to goods and services for their local unit. Their belief was that because nature had endowed women with the ability to create life, they should occupy a position of power that would allow them to protect that function. As the custodians of life, women encouraged deep respect for themselves as mothers, and for Mother Earth, while the main concern of men was the protection of women.

For governance, women selected titular leaders from the male population. A clan mother nominated candidates for chief whom she believed did not want or seek political power. Women then voted to select a chief. He was subject to recall if he displeased the women. The chief remained in power as long as he did not display motives of greed, envy, malice, or lust for power.

For economic purposes, all products brought to the home by a male became the property of the woman. Her power over their use or disposal was absolute.

The cultural possibilities amazed the teenaged Elizabeth Cady, who had previously seen nothing but male domination of all resources and people. As Iroquois historian Sally Roesch Wagner stated, women who observed Oneida culture "caught a glimpse of the possibility of freedom because they knew women who lived liberated lives, women who had always possessed rights beyond their wildest imagination...." The effect of this Peterboro experience on the youthful Elizabeth Cady was colossal and enduring. She must have wondered, *What is wrong with us? Why can women in our families not have similar social power?* This perception launched her into a lifelong pursuit of equitable treatment of women based on their Natural Rights and personhood. Certainly, the influence of the Smith family on this aspect of the reform era is clear. The adult Elizabeth Cady Stanton became probably the most powerful spokesperson for women's rights in the nineteenth century.[4]

One of Cady Stanton's biggest complaints involved the loss of identity faced by a woman when she married. The most egregious and outrageous symbol of this was the loss of her name. As if the loss of her property and income to her husband were not enough, she also had to adopt his identifying name. Cady Stanton likened it to the slave who was forced to adopt his master's last name, saying that being called "Mrs. Henry Stanton" made her feel like a chattel slave whose name reflected the dominance of his owner. "I have very serious objections... to being called Henry," she asserted. And when Gerrit addressed her in a letter as "E.C. Stanton," she critically shot back, "E.C. is no name. Suppose I should write to you Mr. G.S. Fitzhugh. You see, my dear cousin, you have not taken in the whole idea of woman's degradation." She even stated her concern in poetic form for Gerrit:

> Ah! Noble cousin, you'll ne'er scorn
> The griefs that make me rave—
> The crown of <u>Manhood</u> you have worn
> But I, was born a <u>slave</u>."[5]

What this demeaning status led to, she claimed, was the attitude in women of seeing self-denial as being more valuable than self-development. This encouraged women to passively accept their inferior status as being legitimate. She hoped the women working for equitable treatment would set the example of maintaining their prideful identity of name even after marriage. Some who did so, for instance, were Angelina Grimké Weld, Elizabeth Smith Miller, Elizabeth Cady Stanton, and abolitionist Abby Kelley Foster.

A major focus of Cady Stanton's concern about relationships between the sexes was that men had difficulty *feeling* what women felt. How could one feel degradation, she asked, if it had never been a part of his life? Gerrit had boasted that he could sense the feelings of a black man to the extent of calling himself "a colored man." Why could he not, asked Cady Stanton, sense the feelings of a woman, even though he lived in a house full of them? The answer rested in his traditional cultural expectation and acceptance of subservience for women. Women were supposed to be so busy and quiet that they did not need empathy.

Cady Stanton said of men, "A privileged class can never conceive the feelings of those who are born to contempt, to inferiority, to degradation." To drive her point home, she challenged Gerrit to conceive of himself as a woman. "How much complacency would you feel in your womanhood?" This was probably a meaningless question to one who could not conceive of himself in a dress occupying a status lower than head of the household. This was probably true for most males then—and now. What is being referenced here has less to do with sex than with power. Most men were—and are—reluctant to relinquish power in order to live as did a Native American male.[6]

What this male orientation toward power produced was domestic tyranny that was fully supported by political, religious, academic, and economic institutions. Regarding religion, women could not occupy positions of authority in the church, and were expected to be subordinate to men in the home. They were allowed no voice in politics because that realm of activity required knowledge and skills that were supposedly beyond the innate abilities of women. They needed no formal education because the domestic tasks of housekeeping and child rearing did not require it. Because they would not learn any specialized skills, the economic enterprise would not need them.

This nearly total pattern of discrimination left women susceptible to the "protection" of men. "Protection" became a euphemism for dominance, thereby obscuring the power issue. A particularly frustrating aspect of the women's rights movement for those activists working within it was the fact that many women opposed its goals. Those who were against suffrage, for instance, claimed that they had all the rights they needed, and did not want the added responsibility of informed voting. Both Gerrit Smith and Cady Stanton were disgusted with such a stance by women. Cady Stanton called them the "mummies of civilization." In a speech in 1848, she declared:

> "The most discouraging, the most lamentable aspect our cause wears is the indifference, indeed the contempt, with which women themselves regard our movement. When the subject is introduced among our young ladies... it is met by the scornful curl of the lip and by expressions of disgust and ridicule.... They glory in their bondage."

She compared such women to the supposedly happy slave, and asked,

> "Can there be one woman in this nation so ignorant that she really thinks she is already living in the full possession of all the rights that belong to a citizen of a Republic?"

The point being made was that by accepting the status quo, women legitimated their own subservience, thereby inhibiting the women's rights movement and retarding change.[7]

The equation that Cady Stanton made between women and slaves made sense in light of the intensity of discrimination against them, and became substantiated when the apologists for slavery like George Fitzhugh cashed in on that theme.

The difference between Fitzhugh's and Cady Stanton's equation of women with slaves is that, whereas Fitzhugh believed it to be a legitimate equation that needed to be maintained, Cady Stanton believed it to be illegitimate and in need of negation.

Fitzhugh was disgusted with the notion of women's rights. To him, "women's rights" was an oxymoron. He bellowed,

> "Nothing in the signs of the times exhibits in stronger relief the fact that free society is in a state of dissolution..., of demoralization and transition, than this stir about woman's rights.... The husband has a legally recognized property in his wife's services, and may legally control, in some measure, her personal liberty. She is his property and his slave."[8]

Fitzhugh was only stating in written form what most men of that era felt. As he said,

> "A man's wife and children are his slaves, and do they not enjoy... his property?"

Even liberal-thinking males like Gerrit subscribed to this belief to some extent. He expected his son Greene to follow his orders to stop fishing, and to show obedience to Gerrit's attempt to groom him to become a businessman. And regarding his wife, Gerrit believed that Ann should always support him, even if he had committed crimes. Divorce would amount to a breach of contract. Ann, he said,

> "is never to cease from her efforts for my reformation, and she is never to put herself in such circumstances as would disable her from receiving me, should I return to her in penitence."[9]

Cady Stanton knew that Gerrit's talk about the equality of women with men was a bit delusional, and labeled his support as rhetorical and financial. Even so, he did not view Ann as "a slave."

Fitzhugh, however, was nearly absolute in his degradation of women. If men were to relinquish their stranglehold on her potential abilities, they would lose their position of superiority. He maintained that if women ever did advance beyond slave status, men would become their enemies.

"He who would emancipate woman, unless he could make her as coarse and strong in mind and body as man, would be her worst enemy.... Let her exhibit strength and hardihood, and man, her master will make her a beast of burden. So long as she is nervous, fickle, capricious, delicate, diffident, and dependent, man will worship and adore her. Her weakness is her strength, and her true art is to cultivate and improve that weakness."[10]

In response to critics who accused him of encouraging the abuse of women, he cited the work of the New England Puritans during the Salem witch hunt.

"If they hung a few troublesome women, the good that they achieved was more than compensated for by any error they may have committed...."

Fitzhugh saw no good to come from liberating women from their obligations to men.

"Liberty and the unlimited right of private judgment have borne no good fruits, and many bad ones.... We do not set children and women free because they are not capable of taking care of themselves.... [Women] are but grown up children, and liberty is as fatal to them as it would be to children."[11]

In the Smith family, Ann, Elizabeth, Gerrit, and Elizabeth Cady Stanton opposed such bigoted notions of the inferiority of women, and worked in their daily lives to contradict them. The two Elizabeths set examples of independence and feminine power, while Ann and Gerrit supported such moves, but had difficulty carrying them out personally—Ann more so than Gerrit. They all understood that Fitzhugh and the host of those who supported him to some degree were wrong in terms of the liberal, democratic philosophy that underpinned American culture and government. Those facing oppression—especially women and black people—did not want just a patched-up legal system that would allow them to be educated or to vote, but a reformed social system that would guarantee equality. Their vision was like the reality embodied in Oneida Nation social structure, but that ideal did not fit well with the male-dominated power structure preferred by the traditions of Euro-Christian culture.

A concept that strongly reinforced the biased perceptions of women's abilities was that of gender. A frequent mistake is to equate gender with sex. Whereas gender refers to masculine or feminine traits, sex refers to biological equipment inherited at birth. Except for rare cases of hermaphrodism, one inherits either male or female sex organs. The mistake we make is to assume that sex determines masculine or feminine tendencies. When that mistake is interpreted into fact, it appears that females ought to be feminine, and males ought to be masculine. That is, gender characteristics should follow rigidly from sexual facts. This might lead one to believe, as did George Fitzhugh, that all women should be, as he put it, delicate, fickle, diffident, and dependent. That certainly was not the case for Elizabeth Cady, even as a young woman.

Recent research on the origin of gender has produced some fascinating facts. We know that masculinity and femininity in their extremes are on opposite ends of a continuum. We also know that each person exhibits both qualities to some degree in a yin-yang type of mix. Most biological males are masculine, with minor feminine traits; most biological females are feminine with minor masculine traits. But 'most' does not mean 'all'.

The dominant cluster of traits—masculine or feminine—is determined early in fetal development. Neurons in the developing human brain are primed to receive and imprint either masculine or feminine tendencies. Those messages come from hormones produced in gonads which mature later in fetal development. Some of the neuronal receptors in the brain will accept a hormonal message to develop feminine traits, and some will accept messages to develop masculine traits. The balance in the number of these receptors can be skewed to favor either masculine or feminine traits. Because this number is unrelated to future gonad development, one's biological sex may not coincide with gender. The startling conclusion of this research is that "...gender identity cannot be predicted from anatomy.... One cannot deny the profound effects of Testosterone, Estradiol and other steroids on genital differentiation... but gender identity is determined before and persists in spite of these effects."[12]

This research is cited to expose the folly of expecting either sex to be naturally anything behaviorally. Women can be masculine and have no interest in filling a "domestic" role, and men can be feminine and sensitive to the needs of others. Gerrit made this point clearly in his writing. He believed that the "powers of woman to produce the means of subsistence are as great as those of man," and he regarded as dangerous the opinion that men and women were naturally different from one another except in physical ways. Males and females, Smith said, could be legitimately separated where matters of procreation were concerned, but in all other respects, "man is woman, and woman is man." This led to his conclusion that "man and woman are one in their rights, in their responsibilities, in their duties, dignity and destiny."[13]

This kind of thinking shot down the idea that the "domestic sphere" of work is where all women belonged, and challenged the notion that they should be obligated to obey anyone. Those like the Smiths, who favored the women's rights movement, encouraged women to seek avenues of self-expression other than religion, and find sources of identity outside of males. Women like Angelina Grimké, Elizabeth Smith Miller, and Elizabeth Cady Stanton surged into areas of supposedly non-feminine behavior where their function was more significant than the person. Public speaking, dress reform, and voting became more important than looking pretty. Submitting to the power and authority of a dominant male—or any males—should be avoided, or at least minimized.

Even the normally reticent Ann Smith felt justified in flexing some independent muscles. In the early 1860s, she demanded of Gerrit that he permit her to have her own bank account that she could disburse as she saw fit. He conceded, and adjusted to his new state of affairs by writing some cynical poems:

"My husband, says Nancy, I firmly now state
That for what is my own I'll no longer wait.
Of all of my wealth let me now be possest
That I may its income make haste to invest.

A cypher's poor Gerrit—a prime Number One
Is this woman who'll show how things should be done.
It's right when the husband has lost all his force,
That the wife, whip in hand, should drive round the course."

As their newly found sense of freedom developed, women felt the power to put down the broom and pick up the mace. When Elizabeth Smith married Charles Dudley Miller in 1843, she found herself to be in a relationship with a typically insensitive male. For the most part, she adjusted to that situation, with their relationship becoming distant during its later stages. But in 1851 as the movement for women's rights warmed and expanded, she made a bold move in favor of women's rights by adopting the wearing of pants. This move shocked Cady Stanton, who thought that her lifelong friend was conservative and comfortable enough to not make waves. Actually, Elizabeth Smith Miller adopted what came to be called "bloomers" for practical, not political, reasons, but because of her status in an elite and philanthropic reform-oriented family, it became big news.

Her social position included connections with nationally known and powerful human rights activists in both the abolition and women's rights movements, so her actions carried political significance as representing that sphere.

The dress reform issue became a highly visible way of attracting a lot of public attention to both the practical and the political aspects of discrimination against women. At the practical level, the bulky, full-length, hooped dress was awkward to move about in, and because of its many layers, could weigh as much as twenty pounds. Miller stated her logic for changing to something more simple as follows:

"In the spring of 1851, while spending many hours at work in the garden, I became so thoroughly disgusted with the long skirt, that the dissatisfaction—the growth of years—suddenly ripened into the decision that this shackle should no longer be endured. The resolution was at once put into practice. Turkish trousers to the ankle with a skirt reaching some four inches below the knee, were substituted for the heavy, untidy and exasperating old garment."[14]

"I wanted some kind of a dress which would enable me to go up stairs with both hands full in comfort. With my long gown I could not take the baby on one arm and a lamp in the other and go up the stairs without running the risk of being tripped up, which might result in burning the baby, myself, and the house."[15]

Elizabeth Smith Miller was a staunch advocate of dress reform, modeling a pair of bloomers here that became a controversial fashion choice for women—and a symbol in the fight for women's rights—in the mid-19th century.

This practical emphasis by Elizabeth Smith Miller was typical of her orientation toward life. She was apolitical, preferring to avoid the public spotlight. With this daring move, however, she leaped directly into it, igniting some very hot political fuses.

The large dress was preferred by most males as a sign of beauty, but its overriding function was as a sign of inferiority. Its size and weight encouraged female passivity. Lucretia Mott called it "drapery." As a symbol of servitude and inferiority, it was seen as an intentional, male-supported barrier to progress toward freedom and independence. Pants were considered to be a badge of power to be worn by men, and when worn by women became a form of cross-dressing that blurred the boundaries between masculine jurisdiction and feminine subservience. Critics claimed it to be inappropriate for women to "wear the pants" in any social setting.

Because bloomers symbolized female emancipation, press reports of women's rights conventions vilified the participants—both female and male. The Syracuse Daily Courier referred to a "petticoat parliament" attended by "Amazons of the New World." The New York Times noted that "vulgar women" with a "love of notoriety" displayed themselves in bloomers. One attack that tried to substitute humor for viciousness was also in the New York Times. It referred to women's rights activist and bloomer supporter Mary Walker:

> "The other day that curious anthropoid, Miss Dr. Mary Walker, was bitten by an injudicious dog. The thoughtless person on hearing of this incident will, of course, feel some natural pity for the dog [that] will doubtless contract her peculiar insanity.... Had Dr. Walker worn the ordinary garments of her sex, she would not have been bitten...."

When one considers some of the major social issues of the mid-nineteenth century, such as frequent and severe economic depression, and health problems for which primitive medical technology had no cures, the dress reform issue might seem like a minor concern. Maybe in some ways it was, but the splash it made in the social scene was like the mess that might be made by a flat rock landing in a mud puddle at the Sunday school picnic. Everyone felt it. Elated women wondered and dreamed; disgusted men balked and resisted; bigoted journalists bellowed and insulted.

Although the personal and practical effects of the dress reform movement are difficult to perceive, its political effects are not. It provided an explosive impetus to the insertion of women into public life by stimulating their development of self-confidence, optimism, and a power base in organizational structure.

The seeds for this growth of feminine power were planted first in the abolition movement in the 1830s. Shortly after the abolition movement warmed up, women wanted to help. But such "political" activity was outside of the realm of expected female concern or behavior. The early antislavery organizations were exclusively male, and protective of their own power base. Women were denied membership, but allowed to "help" by conducting such domestic-like functions as fundraising and petition drives. Women soon became aware that even these liberal-minded, human rights advocates intended to discriminate against them. Their response was not to fight the entrenched males, but to form their own female anti-slavery societies.

These organizations first appeared in 1833, and the first Women's Anti-Slavery Convention was held in New York City on May 9-12, 1837. It was chaired by Lucretia Mott, with Ann Carroll Smith present as vice president. The significance of the early meetings is that they were the first interracial, public, and politically oriented efforts of American women.

The reaction of the press to females working for public goals was typical. The <u>New York Commercial Advertiser</u> called them "misguided ladies... who put aside their frying pans to debate weighty matters of state." Church organizations expressed regret that women would "bear an obtrusive and ostentatious part in measures of reform."[17]

Two of the early female leaders in the abolition movement were Abby Kelley and Angelina Grimké. As they worked initially for the benefit of the slave, they soon realized their own personal connection to oppression. Kelley noted that,

"We have a good cause to be grateful to the slave for the benefit we have received to ourselves in working for him. In striving to strike his irons off, we found most surely that we were manacled ourselves, not buy <u>one</u> chain only, but by many. In every struggle we have made for him, we find we have been also struggling for ourselves."[18]

Kelley's persistence in securing power for women made for the focus of controversy over the proper role of women in politically oriented organizations. When she was selected as a member of the business committee of the American Anti-Slavery Society in 1840, the result was a split in that organization over whether women should be allowed to become active participants in decision making.

Grimké was another controversial figure when in 1837 she became an effective public speaker on the anti-slavery circuit. Between May and November of that year, she spoke at eighty-seven locations to over 40,000 people. The most significant aspect of her public speaking was that she combined the abolition message with that of women's rights, thus spreading the flames of the emerging women's rights movement.

According to male abolitionists, a major benefit of having women participate in "their" movement was that women would bring with them their stereotypical concern for moral issues. This, they felt, would dilute the potential stigma of practical males being identified with moral issues, and thus be feminized.

An event that roused women to action and prompted them to become involved politically in social issues was the World Anti-Slavery Convention in London, England in 1840. Elizabeth Cady and Henry Stanton attended it as part of their honeymoon. When the British managers of the convention refused to seat the female delegates from the United States, Cady Stanton was outraged. She was obliged to sit in the gallery as a non-participant, where she met the delegate Lucretia Mott

.Their collective disgust with this formal snub that ignored their presence and neglected their significance motivated them to declare their intent to issue a call for a women's rights convention upon their return home.

The influence of the Smith family on Cady Stanton was primary in her decision to make that call. As part of their honeymoon, she and Henry had spent two days with them in Peterboro before departing for London, and when they returned in late December, spent part of the winter living in Peterboro with the Smiths. We can only try to imagine the content of the dinner table and fireside talks. They must have been intensely spiced with ideas about human rights, and plans for future organizations, campaigns, and hopeful successes.

Cady Stanton took a brave and daring first step on February 14, 1854. On that day, she became the first woman to address the testosterone-laced, male dominated New York State Legislature with a message entitled "Women's Rights." Following her speech, an editor of the Albany Register likened it to

"the performances of... the clown in the circus,... or the minstrelsy of gentlemen with blackened faces...," and he chastised "feminine propagandists of women's rights" who seem to be enjoying "the novelty of this new phase of hypocrisy and infidel fanaticism."

He continued:

"People are beginning to inquire how far public sentiment should sanction or tolerate these unsexed women, who would step out from the true sphere of the mother, the wife, and the daughter, and taking upon themselves the duties and the business of men, stalk into the public gaze, and, by engaging in the politics, the rough controversies and trafficking of the world, upheave existing institutions, and overrun all the social relations of life."[19]

Women who were serious about pursuing equality with men fortified themselves against such criticism, strengthened their resolve, and moved on feeling certain that they would succeed. In the 1830s, they participated in organizations of reform related to religion and temperance, and carried the idea of organizational work into the 1840s with increasing numbers of female antislavery societies. They did understand that a networked base of pro-women's rights organizations was necessary for successful pursuit of social change, but were working against the cultural headwind of biased males already in positions of power. Even those men who supported their effort were skeptical of its success.

Gerrit Smith favored equity in the treatment of women throughout his life, but warned cousin Cady Stanton to be prepared for frustration and failure. What he knew was that the traditional pattern of male dominance was rooted in long-standing domestic custom, and reinforced by the overbearing power of religion. This led him to question the efficacy of any quality of effort to produce change, especially because—and this is what enraged Cady Stanton—he felt that the movement was being run by women who were unprepared to lead it successfully. As he put it, the women's rights movement

"is not in the proper hands, and... the proper hands are not yet to be found.... My sorrow is that they who are intent upon it, are not capable of adjusting themselves to it—not high-souled enough to consent to those changes and sacrifices in themselves, in their positions and relations, essential to the attainment of this vital object."

Smith felt that women "in the present age" were incapable of successful political work due to incompetency based in centuries of previous domestic servitude. He fortified his opinion by adding:

"If there is not enough compass of mind and mobility of soul—not enough of strong common sense and bravery and self-sacrifice in our age to furnish the necessary bands of reformers against Intemperance and Slavery, certain it is that it must be left to another age to furnish the reformers who are competent to carry the cause of women to victory. For, it must be remembered that the success of this cause will involve more comprehensive, and radical, and difficult changes than will the success of all those other reforms put together."[20]

This pessimistic opinion was based in Gerrit's practical observation of the population and its prevalent attitudes. The bias against women, he felt, was more intense than the bias against black people, involved a much greater number of people, and was spread over all institutional areas of social life. Also, many women opposed the women's rights movement, thus robbing power from its own base. These facts arranged his human rights priorities in a way that made women not his top concern. "The removal of the political disabilities of race is my first desire, of sex, my second," he told Susan B. Anthony. And to another friend he offered, "Very desirous am I that justice be done to women.... But my first duty is to my colored brothers and sisters."[21]

It seems unfortunate that Gerrit Smith's opinions about the efficacy of reform in the sphere of women's rights was so prophetic. The one issue area that illustrates the glacial rate of progress for the women's rights movement is the decades-long struggle to achieve woman suffrage.

The question of whether or not women should be allowed to vote in the United States exposed a reality that has been an awkward and humiliating part of the culture since its inception: the intense bias of men against equity for women. A fair point to note is that, in a democracy based on written principles of equality and justice for all, no question should arise about the ability of any adult citizen to vote. The fact that "woman suffrage" was such a divisive issue for so long emphasizes the devastating effect of entrenched political power. It is not a surprise that some women felt abused by biased males. What *is* surprising is that the reform efforts persisted for so long in the face of the aggressive assault of hostile, malicious, power-hungry men.

The contributions of the Smith family to the long crusade for woman suffrage may seem to be equivocal, but they are not. All family members supported the issue in principle, but there were times when practical considerations diluted support.

The first serious shout by women for equitable treatment came at Seneca Falls in July of 1848. Elizabeth Cady Stanton and Lucretia Mott had finally produced the Women's Rights Convention that they had discussed in 1840. The Declaration of Sentiments signed at that convention declared "that it is the duty of the women of this country to secure to themselves their sacred right to the elective franchise." There are three points of importance in this statement: 1—all women have this duty, not just white women; 2—voting is a sacred right, not the privilege of a few, but a Natural Right conferred at birth; 3—women would need to do the work themselves against the opposition of men.

At this early stage in the suffrage movement, Gerrit Smith was clear about his stand favoring woman suffrage. One month before the July 1848 Seneca Falls convention, he supported a plan to enfranchise women that was part of the Liberty Party platform, saying,

"This universal exclusion of women [from voting] argues, conclusively, that, not as yet, is there one nation so far emerged from barbarism... as to permit women to rise up to the... level of the human family. It also argues... that Civil Government is so unhappily confounded with these flagrant forms of injustice as to make the thought of woman's participation in it revolting and absurd."[22]

Smith maintained this liberal position regarding woman suffrage through the 1850s. At the 1852 Liberty League Convention in Canastota, he held

"that all persons—black and white, male and female—have equal political rights, and are equally entitled to the protection and advantages of Civil Government."

He repeated this point in an 1857 speech in Milwaukee.[23]

Had it not been for the Civil War, the abolitionists' support of woman suffrage probably would have remained firm. But the prospects for the abolition of slavery and the freedom of black people changed their minds. The obvious fact was that after the war, discrimination against black people would not end, so black males would need the power of the vote to protect themselves from vengeful and powerful white people. Black women, of course, were not considered as potential voters.

Leading Boston abolitionist Wendell Phillips stated the issue clearly. "This hour," he said, "belongs to the Negro.... I say, one question at a time." His point was that because discrimination against women was more intense than discrimination against blacks, if both were included in the same Constitutional amendment, it would not be ratified. Women, therefore, would have to wait until the level of discrimination against them had subsided before expecting the vote.[24]

As previously indicated, Gerrit Smith agreed with Phillips by saying that women were his "second" choice for receiving the vote. Frederick Douglass was an early supporter of women's rights, even attending the 1848 Seneca Falls convention, but he sided with Phillips and Smith on the suffrage issue, saying,

"I do not see how anyone can pretend that there is the same urgency in giving the ballot to woman as to the negro.... When women, because they are women, are hunted down;... when they are dragged from their houses and hung upon lamp-posts; when their children are torn from their arms, and their brains dashed out upon the pavement; when they are objects of insult and outrage at every turn; when they are in danger of having their homes burnt down over their head; when their children are not allowed to enter schools; then they will have an urgency to obtain the ballot equal to our own."[25]

When these men appealed to women to keep quiet regarding their

Frederick Douglass sided with Gerrit Smith in placing a higher priority on the abolition of slavery than the support of women's rights.

From the modern portrait by Joe Flores, commissioned by the National Abolition Hall of Fame & Museum

demands for suffrage, Elizabeth Cady Stanton called them "pathetic." Even Ann Smith disagreed with her husband Gerrit—something she rarely did. In February of 1866, Ann sent to Congress a petition favoring woman suffrage signed by twenty-eight women.[26]

The result of these disagreements was a chasm between former allies—the abolitionists and the women's rights advocates—that lasted for the rest of their lives. Their respect for one another remained, but the women felt betrayed by those abolitionists whom they had dutifully supported. Their reaction was to regroup and pursue their goals without male support. Cady Stanton shouted that "reform" was not enough, and established "The Revolution"—a journal dedicated to women's rights goals. Women coalesced and formed new organizations in a growing and networked power base: the American Equal Rights Association in 1866; the National Woman Suffrage Association and the American Woman Suffrage Association in 1869; these latter two merged in 1890.

Two postwar Constitutional amendments had the potential for enfranchising women. Although the Fourteenth Amendment left room for debate, it did include the word "male" in its specifications for eligible voters, so it was legally interpreted to exclude females. The Fifteenth Amendment specified only that the "vote shall not be denied... on account of race, color, or previous condition of servitude." These amendments were ratified in 1868 and 1870 respectively.

Women argued that because the Fourteenth Amendment did not specifically deny the vote to women, it was grounds for enfranchisement, but male-dominated courts disagreed. They lobbied long but futilely to have the word "sex" included in the list of categories not to be denied the vote in the Fifteenth Amendment, but did not succeed. The point that had become clear in the postwar era was that the end of slavery was no more the end of racism against blacks than acquiring the vote would be the end of sexism against women. In short, the bastion of white male superiority was intact, and that was in part due to the powerful opinions of elite males like Gerrit Smith and Frederick Douglass.

This seeming apostasy on Smith's part was unusual in his lifelong support of progressive and liberal causes. He maintained that his principled support for woman suffrage never waned, but his practical support of it did. After the enfranchisement of black males in 1870, Smith reaffirmed his support of woman suffrage, but because of his—and others'—critically timed pause in support, his concern and apologies came too late.

During the rest of the nineteenth century, women stayed active in their pursuit of suffrage. Certain that the national government would not respond to her demands for the vote, Elizabeth Cady Stanton initiated a grueling campaign to get states to pass suffrage legislation. Her first such futile effort was in the remote, dusty frontier state of Kansas. During her work there, she wrote to Elizabeth Smith Miller, "Oh... the dirt, the food!!" Even at the state level, legislators would not yield. Between 1870 and 1890, women suffrage amendments were defeated by public referendum in eight states.[27]

Another futile attempt was the 1869 submission to Congress of a proposed Sixteenth Amendment to the Constitution that read:

> "The Right of Suffrage in the United States shall be based on citizenship,... and all citizens of the United States... shall enjoy this right equally without any distinction or discrimination whatever founded on sex."

This proposed amendment languished in committee until 1887 when the Senate defeated it by a vote of sixteen in favor, twenty-four opposed, and twenty-six absentions.[28]

One last futile enfranchisement effort by women occurred during the presidential election of 1872. In a brazen act of defiance of federal law, seven women voted in Rochester, New York, one of whom was Susan B. Anthony. She proudly wrote to Cady Stanton that she "had gone and done it!!"

On November 28, all seven women were arrested by Federal Marshal Elisha Keeney on $500 bail, to appear in United States District

Court on January 21, 1873. Anthony's trial of prosecution started on June 18, 1873 in Canandaigua on the charge of having "knowingly, wrongfully, and unlawfully" voted.

The judge was Ward Hunt, referred to by Cady Stanton as "a small-brained, pale faced... man." This was his first criminal case, and he issued the decision of guilty without consulting the jury. "[W]ith remarkable forethought," said Cady Stanton, "he had penned his decision before hearing it."

Anthony was fined $100 plus court costs, to which she immediately responded, "I should never pay a dollar of your unjust penalty." Although Hunt tried to silence her, she said:

"Yes, your honor, I have many things to say; for in your ordered verdict of guilty, you have trampled under foot every vital principle of our government. My natural rights, my civil rights, my political rights, my judicial rights, are all alike ignored."[29]

Although he knew of Anthony's refusal to pay her fine, Gerrit Smith sent her $100 to cover her costs, telling her to use the money as she wished. On March 2, 1874, President Grant directed the Attorney General to forgive Anthony's fine, thereby pardoning her of the crime of having voted.[30]

One last chapter in the story of the Smith family's part in the reform era involves Gerrit and Ann's daughter Elizabeth. Her support of the dress reform movement took place in the 1850s in Peterboro. Although she was always supportive of woman suffrage, her shyness regarding self-expression resulted in her keeping a low social profile. Domestic issues, including her apolitical interest in dress form, occupied her while she resided in Peterboro until 1869.

In 1868, she did write a letter on behalf of women to the National Republican Convention meeting in Chicago in June, asking the party to include in its platform the right of women to vote. In 1869, she was selected as treasurer of the new National Woman Suffrage Association.

She also sought her father's support for women's rights organizations, and for Cady Stanton's new publication, <u>The Revolution</u>.[31]

The major impetus in Elizabeth becoming deeply involved in politically oriented woman suffrage work was the influence of her only daughter, Anne Fitzhugh Miller. Born in Peterboro on March 4, 1856, Anne was very active as a child. She liked to act in stage performances and participated in outdoor sports, even becoming the captain of a Peterboro women's baseball team. She enjoyed learning in school, and cultivated her own garden near Greene's Birdhouse.

The Elizabeth and Charles Miller family moved to a spacious sixty-four-acre estate just one-half mile south of Geneva on the shore of Seneca Lake on July 5, 1869. Anne was thirteen years old. When mature, she became politically active in the women's rights movement, with an intense interest in woman suffrage. Anne and Elizabeth held an annual spring "Piazza Party" on the wraparound porch of their Lochland estate to which they invited leaders of the women's rights movement to speak.

Elizabeth Smith Miller (r) with her daughter, Anne, at Lochland in 1908.
From the author's collection

The Lochland estate on Seneca Lake, where Elizabeth and Anne Miller hosted the 1897 Woman Suffrage Convention.

Courtesy of the Geneva Historical Society

    In November of 1897, the Millers hosted the annual convention of the New York State Woman Suffrage Association at their home in Geneva. The four-day event listed in its program (following pages) addresses from many of the giants in the women's rights movement.

    Stimulated by this convention, Anne and Elizabeth founded the Geneva Political Equality Club on November 30, 1897. Fifty charter members agreed to pursue equity and justice for all persons with emphasis on cooperation among the sexes. This original group consisted of an equal number of men and women "of public spirit and progressive principles." Although open to both men and women, the main emphasis of the GPEC was woman suffrage. Anne was elected as its president in 1898, and served until her death in 1912. In order to maintain a balanced perspective on the issue, Anne even invited anti-woman suffrage persons to speak.

    Anne's work through the GPEC was highly respected, and she was responsible for establishing other political equality clubs in the Central New York communities of Phelps, Clifton Springs, and

The

Twenty-ninth Annual Convention

of the

New York State

Woman Suffrage Association,

Geneva, November 3, 4, 5 and 6, 1897.

Headquarters—The Nester Hotel.

Collins Hall—November 3, 7.45 p. m.
Smith Opera House—November 4 and 5, 9.30 a. m., and 2.30 and 7.45 p. m.

Executive board meetings at The Nester.
All other meetings open to the public.
Entrance fee of ten cents on Thursday and Friday Evenings.

"Taxation without representation is tyranny."

Officers of the

New York State Woman Suffrage Association.

President—MARIANA W. CHAPMAN,
160 Hicks St., Brooklyn.

Vice Pres't at Large—ELIZABETH BURRILL CURTIS,
West New Brighton, Staten Island.

Recording Secretary—MARY THAYER SANFORD,
20 James St., Rochester.

Corresponding Secretary—ISABEL HOWLAND, Sherwood.
Treasurer—KATE S. THOMPSON, 39 Allen St., Jamestown.

Auditors: { JEAN BROOKS GREENLEAF, Rochester.
ELIZA WRIGHT OSBORNE, Auburn.

Chairman of Organization Committee—HARRIET MAY MILLS, 926 W. Genesee St., Syracuse.
Chairman of Legislative Committee—MARY HILLARD LOINES, 6 Garden Place, Brooklyn.
Chairman of Press Committee—ELNORA M. BABCOCK, Dunkirk.
Chairman of Industrial Committee—HARRIETT A. KEYSER, 252 W. 95th St., New York.
Chairman of Finance Committee—HENRIETTA M. BANKER, Ausable Forks.
Chairman of Committee on Work Among Children—J. MARY PEARSON, Auburn.
Chairman of Railroad Committee—JULIE R. JENNEY, Everson Bldg., Syracuse.

Above and facing page: The program for the 1897 Woman Suffrage Convention in Geneva.

WEDNESDAY, NOVEMBER 3.
AFTERNOON, 3.00-5.00.
Executive Board Meeting at The Nester.

EVENING, 7.45-9.45.

MUSIC,	MANDOLIN CLUB
PRAYER,	PRESIDENT JONES, Hobart College, Geneva
ADDRESS OF WELCOME,	MR. M. F. BLAINE, Geneva
RESPONSE,	{ MRS. MARIANA W. CHAPMAN, Brooklyn, *President New York State Women Suffrage Association.*
ADDRESS,	{ MRS. LILLIE DEVEREAUX BLAKE, New York, *President New York City League.*
ADDRESS,	{ MISS ALICE STONE BLACKWELL, Boston, *Editor of the Woman's Journal.*
ADDRESS,	{ MISS SUSAN B. ANTHONY, Rochester, *President National American Women Suffrage Association.*

THURSDAY, NOVEMBER 4.
MORNING, 9.30-12.00.

MINUTES,	
.	MRS. MARY THAYER SANFORD
ANNOUNCEMENT OF COMMITTEES: Credentials, Resolutions, Finance, Courtesies.	
ROLL CALL OF COUNTIES.	
REPORT OF EXECUTIVE COMMITTEE, MRS. MARIANA W. CHAPMAN	
REPORT OF CORRESPONDING SECRETARY, MISS ISABEL HOWLAND	
REPORT OF TREASURER,	MRS. KATE S. THOMPSON
REPORT OF FINANCE COMMITTEE,	
	MRS. HENRIETTA M. BANKER, *Chairman*
INTRODUCTION OF FRATERNAL DELEGATES.	
COUNTY REPORTS.	

AFTERNOON, 2.00-3.00.

MINUTES.	
REPORT OF CREDENTIALS COMMITTEE.	
ELECTION OF OFFICERS.	

AFTERNOON, 3.00-4.30.

MUSIC—Piano Solo,	MISS FOWLE, Geneva
PRAYER,	REV. MR. BALLOU, Geneva
ADDRESS,	{ MISS HARRIET MAY MILLS, Syracuse, *Chairman of Organization Committee.*
ADDRESS,	MR. CHARLES HEMIUP, Geneva
ADDRESS,	MRS. MARY LEWIS GANNETT, Rochester
QUESTION BOX.	REV. DR. REMICK, Geneva

EVENING, 7.45-9.45.
(Ten cents admission.)

MUSIC,	BRADWOOD QUARTETTE, Geneva
PRAYER,	REV. LANSING BAILEY, Geneva
ADDRESS,	MRS. MARY SEYMOUR HOWELL, Albany
ADDRESS,	MISS JULIA R. JENNEY, Syracuse
ADDRESS,	{ MISS HARRIETTE A. KEYSER, New York, *Chairman Industrial Committee.*
ADDRESS,	MR. W. SMITH O'BRIEN, Geneva
ADDRESS,	REV. ANNIS FORD EASTMAN, Elmira

FRIDAY, NOVEMBER 5.
MORNING, 9.30-12.00.

MINUTES.	
REPORT OF COMMITTEE ON WORK AMONG CHILDREN,	
	MRS. J. MARY PEARSON, *Chairman*
REPORT OF LEGISLATIVE COMMITTEE,	
	MRS. MARY HILLARD LOINES, *Chairman*
REPORT OF INDUSTRIAL COMMITTEE,	
	MISS HARRIETTE A. KEYSER, *Chairman*
REPORT OF ORGANIZATION COMMITTEE,	
	MISS HARRIET MAY MILLS, *Chairman*
PLAN OF WORK.	
PLACE OF HOLDING NEXT CONVENTION.	
CONSTITUTIONAL AMENDMENTS.	

AFTERNOON, 2.00-4.30.

COUNTY REPORTS.	
REPORT OF RESOLUTIONS COMMITTEE.	
REPORT OF PRESS COMMITTEE, ELNORA M. BABCOCK, *Chairman*	

EVENING, 7.45-9.45.

MUSIC—Chorus	UNION SCHOOL CHILDREN
PRAYER,	REV. A. H. BROADWAY, D.D., Geneva
ADDRESS,	MRS. MARY E. CRAIGIE, Brooklyn
ADDRESS,	MRS. IDA A. HARPER, Indianapolis, Ind.
ADDRESS,	DR. WILLIAM H. JORDAN, Experiment Station, Geneva
ADDRESS,	{ REV. ANNA HOWARD SHAW, Philadelphia, *Vice-President at Large, National American W. S. A.*

SATURDAY, NOVEMBER 6.
MORNING, 9.00.
EXECUTIVE BOARD MEETING AT THE NESTER.

Honeoye. Her Geneva club was the largest in New York State, reaching a membership of 362 in 1907. Also in 1907, Anne and Elizabeth again hosted the annual convention of the New York State Woman Suffrage Association at their Geneva home. Activities associated with the GPEC attracted community residents while pursuing the goal of woman suffrage.

One of the major goals of the Millers was the education of women. Pursuant to that, they founded the Elizabeth Smith Miller Study Club in 1906 for young people over the age of sixteen. It met twice each month to study the lives of successful people. Its fifty students were mostly women. This club spawned the Political Equality Study Class to pursue issues related to woman suffrage. Elizabeth's commitment to educating women prompted her to donate thousands of dollars to the establishment of William Smith College for Women in Geneva in 1908. A building on that campus is named in her honor. She also made orange marmalade to sell as a means of raising funds for scholarships for women attending William Smith College.

Anne also became involved in legislative activity by appearing before legislative committees in the state capital of Albany in support of woman suffrage. Both Anne and Elizabeth testified before the New York State Judiciary Committee in 1899, and both worked through the legislative committee of the New York State Woman Suffrage Association, often meeting at their Lochland estate.

A regular feature of the work of people striving for woman suffrage was frustration. Male-dominated state and national legislatures were mired in discriminative tradition and drunk on their own power. The result was that none of the female members of the Smith family that we have studied herein ever voted. As an example of the frustration they faced, until 1917, the New York State Constitution specified that only males could vote. A bill to remove the word "male" from Article Two, Section One was submitted to the legislature every year for decades with no success. In 1911, the year that Elizabeth Smith Miller died, it came out of committee for a floor vote for the first time since 1895. It was defeated in the Senate. In spite of there being one hundred fifty-five woman suffrage organizations in New York State with over fifty-five thousand members, the state legislature would not hear them.

As a final note, a symbol of the blatant hypocrisy that paralyzed progress toward woman suffrage is the Statue of Liberty. When it was unveiled in the New York City harbor in 1886, women suffragists called it

> "a gigantic lie, a travesty, and a mockery.... It is the greatest sarcasm of the nineteenth century [to represent liberty as a woman] while not one single woman throughout the length and breadth of the Land is yet in possession of political liberty."[32]

~ 5 ~

Issues Supportive of Reform

The two giant issues that dominated during the nineteenth century reform era were the abolition of slavery and women's rights. These reform efforts absorbed the passionate energies of moral reformers like the Smiths, prevailed at dinner table and parlor discussions, and guided the direction of social organizational work and even the establishment of political parties.

There were also corollary efforts within other issue areas that were supportive of all reform activity. Two such areas that deserve attention are the support of educational efforts that targeted the discriminative effects of social bias, and the pursual of temperance in alcohol consumption to encourage reasoned and moderate behavior.

As noted in chapter four, Elizabeth Smith Miller's support of education for women was a major focus of her philanthropy. She knew that a solid knowledge base of history and cultures would prime women for effective work in the women's rights movement, and spent much money and personal, practical effort to support women's formal education, and to develop educational opportunities for women.

One of Gerrit Smith's early interests after graduation from college was the development of formal education for young black males. In 1826, at a very early stage in the growth of his empathic mind, he proposed the establishment in Peterboro of a school based on Christian principles to educate black male youth in preparation for sending them to Africa as representatives of the American Colonization Society with the hope that they would help Christianize Africa. This

is obviously an ethnocentric and biased motive, but Smith was young, and had just been converted to Christianity through the diligent efforts of his wife and former mother-in-law. Elizabeth wrote to her grandfather Peter Smith in April of 1832,
> "They have all been preparing things for the black School which is to be held in this place."[1]

Gerrit Smith's manual labor school for black males opened on May 1, 1834 with fifteen students in attendance. He received letters of approval for his idea from Samuel Eli Cornish and John Brown Russwurm, two black abolitionists and journalists who approved of colonization.[2] The New Haven Journal of Freedom reported that,
> "The School is established in the belief that it is the duty of the whites to elevate the condition in character of the colored people.... Mr. Smith provides, at his own expense, instructors, books, stationary, rooms, bedding, fuel, lights, and boarding.... The student is expected to labor four hours daily in some agricultural or mechanical employment.... It is intended that the School shall afford advantages for obtaining either a good common or classical education."

One of the students at the Peterboro school wrote to William Lloyd Garrison about the school and his "sincere friend" Gerrit Smith.
> "He has established the school not with a view to raise up statesmen, but a useful class of public-spirited and pious young men, who will go forth and take an active part in the great works of moral reform."

The school closed in 1836, probably as a result of Smith's withdrawal from the American Colonization Society. He had become aware of and disillusioned with its racist goal of deporting free black people to Africa, and joined the growing American Anti-Slavery Society. Gerrit's abolitionist friend Beriah Green, an advocate of immediate abolition, had visited Gerrit to convince him that "colonization tends to perpetuate slavery, prejudice, hatred, and all uncharitableness towards the unfortunate colored man."[3]

Because he was concerned about the quality of Peterboro residents, Smith funded the establishment of an educational academy there in 1851. Its purpose was to "educate the understanding and the heart most wisely, and promote refinement of manners." His reference to the "heart" indicates his intent to develop feeling persons. The Academy served about one hundred students per year.[4]

In 1853, Gerrit provided twenty-five thousand dollars for the building of a public library in the City of Oswego. Because of his large business operations there, he felt an obligation to the quality of life of Oswego residents, so he decided to contribute to their intellectual development through the library.

Other efforts to support interracial education were scattered throughout Gerrit's professional career. In 1825, he became a trustee of his alma mater Hamilton College. He resigned that position in 1837 over a dispute with the college administration regarding antislavery activity by students on campus. In the 1830s, he funded the interracial Oneida Institute in Whitestown (now Whitesboro), New York where Beriah Green was its president. In 1839, he gifted the interracial Oberlin College in Ohio with twenty-one thousand acres of land and two thousand dollars in cash to use as it saw fit in supporting its abolition-related efforts. In 1858, Gerrit purchased the interracial New York Central College in McGrawville (now McGraw) in order to save it from bankruptcy, but three years later, the school failed again, and closed.

During the 1856-1874 period, Smith donated money to several interracial colleges including Berea College in Kentucky, Hampton Agricultural Institute in Virginia, Dartmouth College in New Hampshire, and Howard University in Washington, D.C. He also donated to coeducational work at the Ladies Domestic Seminary in Clinton, New York, and made a large donation of ten thousand dollars to Hamilton College in Clinton just before he died in 1874.[5]

The reasoning behind the Smiths' support of education is sound. Higher levels of education correlate positively with more liberal thought patterns, so it offered a way of reducing bias generally. Also, oppressed people needed self-confidence, knowledge, and skills to help them withstand abuse and actualize equality with others.

Another issue that relates to the moral quality of life of all people is the consumption of alcoholic beverages. In that they can alter consciousness, the tendency for one to commit acts that one would not normally commit is raised. As Gerrit Smith put it, bars where people go to drink are "the great manufactory of incendiaries, madmen and murderers." And when people get drunk, they "swear, and lie, and steal, and murder."[6]

Writing to a friend in 1845, Smith warned, "We have a great work to do in our unhappy country. There are not only three millions of slaves to deliver, but more than half a million drunkards." And at one time, he was one of them. As a student at Hamilton College, he had experienced the effects of alcohol firsthand. He wrote in 1841, "I formerly drank intoxicating liquors, and several times I got drunk. But a merciful God showed me my sin in this respect...."[7]

It is curious that Smith spent so much energy, time, and resources on such a futile effort as temperance, but perhaps this seems so only after having witnessed the ineffectual federal attempt to legislate prohibition in the twentieth century. In the 1800s when he took up the cause, he believed that a more perfectly moral society was possible, and that minimizing the use of alcohol would hasten it. It was his vision of a more equitable social world that drove him on in spite of public apathy and frustration. In the face of obvious failure, he still refused to quit. Such was the mind of many of the overly optimistic—and perhaps naïve—reformers.

The issue of the temperate use of alcohol was a perfect fit for Gerrit's mind. It melded the moral vagueries of religion with real world action in a type of practical holiness that made him feel good. And the public seemed receptive. The local evangelism of the Second Great Awakening revival episode had primed people to accept simple answers to complex problems, and Gerrit was good at providing them. His practical logic simply stated that people who drink to excess, do and say stupid things and cannot be trusted. This makes drinking sinful, so—stop drinking!

Smith never did advocate total abstinence from alcohol, just temperate use of it. His major focus was against the sale of liquor by-the-drink in "dram shops" or bars. "I would not have the Legislature enact laws to restrain the traffic in intoxicating drinks." What he did want to accomplish was to prevent the sale of liquor licenses by local boards of excise. If successful, that would stop the sale of liquor by-the-drink.[8]

"Does our party mean to prohibit the importation of intoxicating liquors, or the manufacture of them, or the use of them in families? No! But our enemies will say that we mean to prohibit them all. It is dramselling only that it means to prohibit...."[9]

One problem with Smith's emphasis on taverns and bars was that the public saw it as class bias: middle- or upper-class people could afford to purchase large volumes of liquor for consumption at home, whereas poor people could afford only a few drinks at a time. Greene Smith criticized his father as he wrote about an upcoming temperance meeting in Morrisville. "I hope you will have a good meeting... and do good without perhaps achieving what you desire." Greene's cynicism echoed the public's perception of Gerrit's position:

"The distinction which you draw between the evils of the dramshop and the evils of the wholesale liquor store where a man may buy a barrel of rum to drink in his own house, is simply a distinction between the poor and the rich."

Greene's drinking posed an interesting problem for Gerrit, as did his challenge to Gerrit's stand against dram shops. To quote Greene at length,

"Many a man...is driven by an ill mannered wife to the dramshop, she refusing to allow liquor in the house.... [And] the rich man, who can afford it, drinks at home while the poor man, who only has a small amount of money at a time, has to resort to the dramshop."

Greene challenged his father's claim that dram shop drunkards were a worse threat than those produced at home. "What difference does it make if a man drink a pint of rum in a dram shop, at home, at sea, in a church or in a gaming house? The liquor is the same.... There seem to me to be several reasons for the dram shop drinking appearing to be worse, tho' I cannot see that it is worse."[10]

It is likely that Greene was, in part, defending his own behavior, which was a painful anomaly for Gerrit to see in his own family.

Gerrit realized that the closing of the dram shops would be a form of discrimination against the poor, but he rationalized it by claiming that it was what the poor needed. In a letter to Vice President Schuyler Colfax in 1870, he wrote, "But let the poor rejoice that their poverty disables them from sharing in this power. Let them prefer being poor to being liquor drinkers...."

Smith's arguably class-biased prejudice against dram shops produced an obsession that caused him to ignore principles of equal rights as he lashed out at poor people who frequented bars and the owners who operated them. An interesting twist in Gerrit's temperance rules was that he did not consider wine to be an intoxicating beverage. It was present in his house for several reasons. He sometimes served it to guests. After a visit to his home by three elite ladies, he wrote to them:

"We thank you that you came this way
To cheer our hearts this chilly day.
We lack not wine when you are nigh.
We'll drink your words and so get high."[11]

Ann appreciated wine with her meals, and Elizabeth used it in some of her recipes. In 1875, Elizabeth published a cookbook titled In The Kitchen which reflected what she saw as a major theme of her life—domestic elegance. The book contains approximately thirteen hundred recipes arranged in twenty-seven categories occupying five-hundred and fifty-six pages.

Regarding the use of wine, Elizabeth wrote, "I do not reject wine nor, in many cases, brandy [in my recipes], but am happy to... give substitutes for them...."[12]

Because wine consumption was a regular part of life for some in the Smith household, one of Gerrit's old college friends, Fletcher N. Haight, helped Gerrit replenish his stock.

"I have ordered to Charles Miller (Gerrit's son-in-law who lived next door) a case of assorted California wine. I intend this for your wife, but you being so long and consistently a temperance man I do not send to your address.... Tell your wife she must drink my health... as I will not ask you to imbibe."[13]

Obviously, the Smith family members were not in agreement regarding participation in the temperance reform effort. There were even times when Gerrit put it aside for a while. It depended upon what other issues became more urgent. His first interest in temperance reform appeared in 1826. The American Society for the Promotion of Temperance was founded that year in Boston. When the New York State Temperance Society was organized in 1829, Gerrit gave it enthusiastic support. The movement found fertile ground in New York state. By 1830, there were six-hundred temperance organizations with over one hundred thousand members in New York.[14]

Gerrit was a popular temperance speaker, and received many invitations to attend local meetings, and state and national conventions. Surprisingly, he attended the temperance gatherings more often than political ones. Between 1830 and 1850, he participated in dozens of such meetings throughout the northeast. He usually told those who invited him to speak at political conventions that the "press of business" was too intense to allow him to take time away from Peterboro. But the temperance call stimulated him to travel.

At the local level in Peterboro, Smith worked on individuals to stop drinking. In the mid-1820s, there was a hotel/tavern at the east end of the Peterboro green that sold hard liquor. To counteract its effects on local people, Gerrit built a "temperance hotel" on his property at the west end of the green in 1827. Due to lack of patronage, it was closed in 1833. It reopened in 1845 to operate on temperance principles, but failed again. Gerrit also established a temperance hotel in Oswego that experienced the same difficulties as did the one in Peterboro. The significance of these hotel efforts lies in their illustration of the radical steps taken by Smith to curtail the sale of liquor, but even such drastic measures did not work.

Another of Smith's tactics to change drinking behavior was to convince a person of the sinfulness of drinking, and have him sign a pledge to desist. One such pledge is shown here:

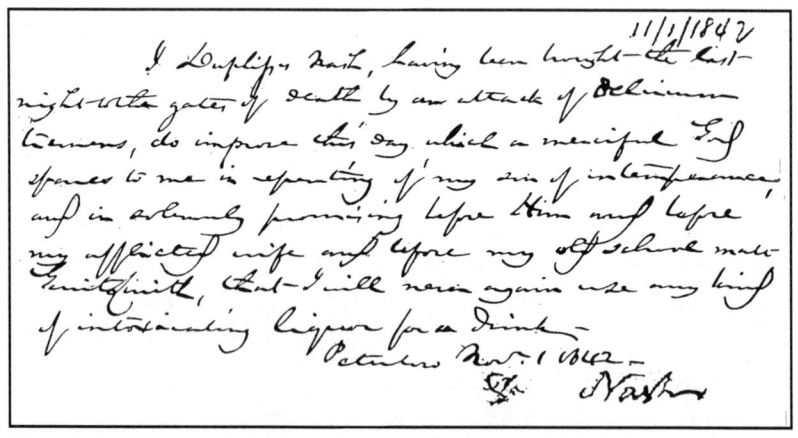

This pledge, written by Gerrit Smith and signed by a friend named Duplissis Nash, represents the kind of personal work Smith did in temperance. It reads,
"I, Duplissis Nash, having been brought—the last night—to the gates of death by an attack of delirium tremens, do improve this day which a merciful God spares to me in repenting of my sin of intemperance, and in solemnly promising before Him and before my afflicted wife and before my old school mate Gerrit Smith, that I will never again use any kind of intoxicating liquor for a drink.

Peterboro Nov. 1 1842
—
D Nash"

In 1841, Gerrit helped to organize the Reformed Drunkards' Society of the Town of Smithfield. Duplissis Nash was most likely one of its members, although its title does not make it sound like a prestigious membership.[15]

Smith felt constant frustration about his decades of work for temperance. He did pause in such efforts between 1852 when he was elected to Congress, in 1865 when the Civil War ended. During those years, he concentrated on the abolition of slavery. But when the war was over, he mounted his temperance steed once more to charge off into the moral abyss. It is difficult to determine whether his biggest frustration was in the wide social field or at home, for this was the one issue area with which his family did not agree to support him fully. Even so, he could not resist the challenge it posed, or relinquish his hope that he could do something about it.

Gerrit Smith's efforts at temperance did bear fruit locally. In 1851, Peterboro resident Henry Campbell wrote to his sister,

"We are completely Totalists in Smithfield as there is not a license granted or a drop sold for anything I know except for medicinal purposes anywhere in town...."[16]

It is probably because of the long-ago influence of Gerrit that the Town of Smithfield, New York is mostly a 'dry town today.

Epilogue

Discrimination hurts! Actually, discrimination against any person for any reason stinks. This is the message that the Smith family left for us as their legacy, and describes the way that they lived their lives. Empathy was their guiding value for relating to other people; empathy being the ability to sense another person's feelings to the extent of identifying with and understanding that person.

When one is being discriminated against, they do not need to be told so—they *feel* it. For the Smiths, feelings produced facts. For most of us, it is the other way around. Think of it this way: if your own perspective on life, and your own feelings are reasonable and logical to you, why would the same not be true for other people? If this makes sense, then other persons' positions deserve as much attention and credibility as one's own.

It is this attitude that resulted in the intense empathy modeled by the Smiths. Their ability to sense others' feelings may have been rooted in a caring gene, but certainly was cultivated through their belief in universal "personhood"—the conviction that everyone inherits equal, natural rights to fair treatment. This belief expressed the Golden Rule that one should treat others as one prefers to be treated; others' feelings are prioritized as being equal in importance to one's own. This is an essential quality of political liberalism, a position held consistently by the Smith family. Such unselfishness allows one to love all people because everyone else is, in essence, like oneself.

When strangers visited the Smith home in Peterboro, they felt dignified and respected because their feelings and perspectives were perceived as valid and were honored. To meet Gerrit and Ann Smith was to feel that the most important person present was yourself, not them. This was an extraordinary accomplishment for an aristocratic family that had ample opportunity amid a huge resource base to live a selfish, luxurious, and materialistic life. Their humility broke down divisions of class, race, sex, age, or any other characteristic, and emphasized the similarity among all persons. No one felt alienated or unworthy.

They lived in the nineteenth century when most communication among people was face-to-face. The Smiths never saw a telephone, a car, or a typewriter. To communicate with someone, they did it in their home, or traveled to see someone, or wrote them a personal letter. Today, electronics separates people from one another's feelings, and legitimates social and physical distances that produce isolation. To communicate with the Smiths was to see their eyes, hear their tone of voice, experience a vigorous handshake or hug, and feel good, knowing that your own opinions were taken seriously and incorporated into their plans for building a society that would offer to all people an equal chance to succeed.

"Reform" was the technique of action that characterized the era. Their parental generation had been effectual in revolutionary ways. As American colonists, they had defied centuries of tradition and the most powerful military force on earth to declare independence and the primacy of democracy. Now, in the nineteenth century, it was time to reform the original institutions of the new nation to reflect more perfectly what the bold statements of the founders had declared as their intentions.

The social realities of early nineteenth century life betrayed previously stated principles of living that were based in equality and justice for all people. The ideals of Jefferson and Madison were dashed on the shoals of slavery and the inferiority of women. The Smiths' generation viewed it as their responsibility to bring the idea of equality to fruition, but to do so, they would need to break the backbone of southern culture.

Based on the fiction of inherent inequality, southern institutions supported a caste system of aristocracy over poverty that permeated every aspect of life—even in the North. Intentional discrimination founded in entrenched prejudice governed social life, and even dominated both state and national governmental policy. "The Slave Power" ruled.

Those who wished to reform corrupt social institutions worked between 1830 and 1865 in a moral drama played out by intellectual giants of all social classes who dedicated their resources and their lives to an idea with a level of passion and commitment perhaps not seen since. Their emotions led to action that changed the structure of society as they stirred the mire of conservatism and altered the dominant thoughts and goals of whole institutions like religion, politics, and business, resulting in a giant step toward the achievement of our stated national purpose of equitable treatment of all persons.

The reformers were certainly implied in British Prime Minister Winston Churchill's World War II statement, "Never was so much owed by so many to so few." As radical activists, they persisted beyond reason against formidable odds to reweave the fabric of our attitudes toward one another. In that process, they not only reformed existing institutions but also built new ones to pursue their goals. In this process, the Smith home in Peterboro became a "safe house"—a therapeutic center for the treatment of abused human rights workers, and a place of protection and aid for those escaping from the trap of slavery or abusive relationships. Also, they established new institutions locally to help the oppressed.

They founded one of the first formal schools in the nation for African-Americans; a church free of sectarian dogma that successfully united the human rights efforts of both religion and politics; a political party committed to implementing equality among previously segregated portions of a diverse population; a home for destitute children dedicated to alleviating the effects of poverty; a temperance hotel devoted to minimizing the effects of the consumption of alcohol within human relationships, and they provided paid employment and property for former slaves in Peterboro, and even developed one scheme to enfranchise some black males through gifts of large plots of land.

The Madison County Children's Home in Peterboro, from a late-1800s postcard. *From the author's collection*

To accomplish all this, the Smiths maintained an upbeat, optimistic attitude, and an undying faith in the intelligence and reasonableness of the general public to see the need for moral change, and be willing to help implement it. They envisioned the actualization of the utopian scene where no bias leads to true liberty and equality.

The frustrations they faced in this work were monumental, yet they refused to feel defeated. As such, they can be perceived as being either heroic or pathetic, but one cannot deny the fact that they tried to equalize the score of the social game by changing its rules. The one aspect of their thought that never faded was their hope that every person would feel dignity. But hope alone cannot produce a new reality, so they felt frustration in trying to make oppression real to someone who has never felt it, or freedom seem necessary to someone who has never lived without it.

The relevance of the work of Ann, Gerrit, Elizabeth, and Greene should be easy to see in today's world, almost a century and a half after they all died. With ultraconservative political leaders like United

States President Donald J. Trump, and English Prime Minister Boris Johnson at the helm, the social ship has once again foundered in bigoted waters. The issues of racism, sexism, and environmental degradation still exist with such intensity that, were the Smiths with us, they would know where to work.

Our craving for laudable human symbols like Harriet Tubman and Sojourner Truth attest to our awareness of the twin tragedies of racism and sexism, and we trust that future leaders will not be bigoted people who exhibit greed, exploitation, and a lust for power. In the words of African-American leader Martin Luther King, Jr., "The arc of the moral universe is long, but it bends toward justice." Most certainly, the Smiths' journey through life followed that arc, and some tangible effects of their legacy can be seen in Peterboro today.

The Gerrit Smith Estate was designated as a National Historic Landmark by the United States Department of the Interior in 2001, and presently hosts many human rights-oriented events and public tours annually. The Smith Land Office where Peter and Gerrit conducted business is recognized on the National Register of Historic Places. The National Abolition Hall of Fame and Museum was established in Peterboro in 2004, and regularly inducts members nominated by the public, and conducts seminars on abolitionists with the aid of academic scholars from locations throughout the United States.

A twenty-five-year run of Peterboro's annual Civil War Weekend celebrated the connections between John Brown, Gerrit Smith's philanthropy, and the abolition of slavery. The current annual Emancipation Day celebration continues that theme. The annual Elizabeth Smith Miller Tea celebrates her legacy in women's rights and strives to aid in voter registration of youth. An annual Gerrit Smith Birthday Celebration in early March commemorates his human rights work with invited guest speakers and tours of the National Abolition Hall of Fame and Museum, and the Gerrit Smith Estate National Historic Landmark.

Certainly the legacy left by the Smith family at the local level is impressive, but it reaches further than that. Visitors to these new institutions in Peterboro acquire a clear sense of the relevance of the reformers' work in the nineteenth century to similar issues we face today. In the last few decades, research on the antislavery movement has exploded. This indicates a recognition of the relevance of the focus and ideas of the abolitionists for giving direction and inspiration to us. And there are some people, especially young people, who are listening.

As the poet Robert Frost aged, he said, "Now that I am old, my teachers are the young." There are reasons to be optimistic about the possibility that the maturing generation of "millennials" born between 1981 and 1996 will rekindle the passion of the nineteenth century reformers and initiate soon a new age of liberal policy that will deal actively with bigotry, oppression, and environmental degradation. Time magazine correspondent Charlotte Alter his researched this new generation. They are the largest living generation, and will soon be the largest voting group. They tend to hold liberal attitudes, and will produce what Altar calls a "progressive youthquake."

As they grow to maturity, millennials learned of the disturbing issues of bigotry, inequality, and economic depression, and faced the reality of long wars, crushing student debt, and environmental inertia. Research has shown that events experienced between the ages of fourteen and twenty-four have roughly triple the impact on one's political opinions compared to events experienced later in life. The result is that 57% of millennials identify with liberal causes. Worldwide, they are protesting against capitalism and corruption in Chile, Iraq, Lebanon, Hong Kong, Iran, and India. They are forcing current conservative leaders to confront the perils of inaction, and are unwilling to work for change from the fringes of current power structures. They want the power themselves.

In the United States, they have inherited the largest national debt ever, an underfunded Social Security program, skewed income distribution, increasing gun violence, and a human population so far over Earth's carrying capacity that problems of ocean pollution, climate change, and a nearly uncontrollable spread of viral diseases are everyday concerns. They feel betrayed by previous generations who have squandered resources that they and their children will need, as they failed to plan for anyone but themselves.

The ethnic composition of the millennial generation is diverse. They are empathic enough to listen to and learn others' points of view, their ideas are progressive and socially liberal—and they vote! 42% of millennials voted in the 2018 midterm elections. That is double the rate of such voters in previous elections, and 60% of those under thirty plan to vote regularly in future elections.

This generation is skilled at networking through social media to build social movements, and eager to accept responsibility for implementing change. In 2018, twenty of them were elected to Congress. Social change movements they support include Black Lives Matter, the Green New Deal, and a brand of "democratic socialism" that advocates governmental provision for universal healthcare, daycare for children, and climate care. Their enormous appetite for social media fuels progress toward political success and the pursual of these goals. And rather than just electoral success, they are aiming toward systemic change in the ways we perceive and react to people and issues. They see undrinkable water in Flint, Michigan, and unbreathable air in Beijing as symptoms of brutal carelessness on the part of profit-seeking leaders.

Examples of the millennials' frustration are worth hearing. Eighteen-year-old Jade Hameister, an Australian explorer, writes that "The world is severely out of balance, thanks to the historic oppression of feminine power." There are one hundred and thirty million young women in today's world who are not in school. The failure to educate women is tragic for world peace and environmental health because women tend to be better caretakers than men.

Twenty-year-old Emma Gonzalez has become a gun control advocate after surviving the 2018 mass shooting at Marjory Stoneman Douglas High School in Parkland, Florida. Her perception of current United States political leadership is worth quoting at length:

"The youth of this world are watching you destroy our lives before they have begun. We are losing our futures, our sanity, and our lives, all because you want more money and more power....

"If you are in a position of power, you need to aim to make the world a better place for everyone living here, not just yourself and your donors. That means fewer guns, less plastic, more therapy, more education. Stop investing in nonrenewable resources and police institutions and private prisons, and start investing in health care and education. Stop allowing violence to persist and being shocked when the youth are softer and gentler than you. Stop utilizing the abusive and manipulative systems that were created for you. Instead, help people of color, women, LGBT+ people, young people, disabled and differently abled people, and immigrants obtain an education, food, clean water, safe housing, jobs, health care and political power.

If you really want to change the way we live our lives, ask us what problems we face and how we think we should solve them, and maybe listen this time. We need positive change, and if you don't make it happen, we will."[1]

These words sound as if they came from Ann and Gerrit Smith! Perhaps there is pending an honest and sincere rebirth of reform efforts. In 1963 as our country was celebrating the one-hundredth anniversary of Lincoln's Emancipation Proclamation, racial activist James Baldwin wrote that "the country is celebrating one hundred years of freedom one hundred years too soon." Let us hope that by 2063, new generations will have carried the torch of moral reform closer to the finish line.

The Smiths carried that torch throughout the nineteenth century. When it eventually reached us in the 1960s, we were mounting a new charge against prejudice in the Civil Rights Movement that, through folk singers Peter, Paul, and Mary still asked,

"How many years must some people exist
before they're allowed to be free?
How many times can a man turn his head
and pretend that he just doesn't see?
...How many ears must one person have
before he can hear people cry?"

Epilogue

The Smiths provided for us the model of people who saw, and heard, and cried—and acted. They knew that prejudice always tells more about the person who holds it than it tells about the person at whom it is aimed. They saw arrogance and tried to soften it. They saw prejudice and tried to counter it.

They saw anger and tried to mitigate it. With these actions, they helped individuals deal with the problems in their lives, and feel better about being who they were, while at the same time building institutions to fight for moral improvement on a national scale. They cared about the conditions of oppressed people, and tried to alleviate their burdens.

It seems proper that we toast the Smith family with a glass of cold water, and hope that their shining spirit of benevolence will kindle a spark of caring in us.

The Smith Family Tree

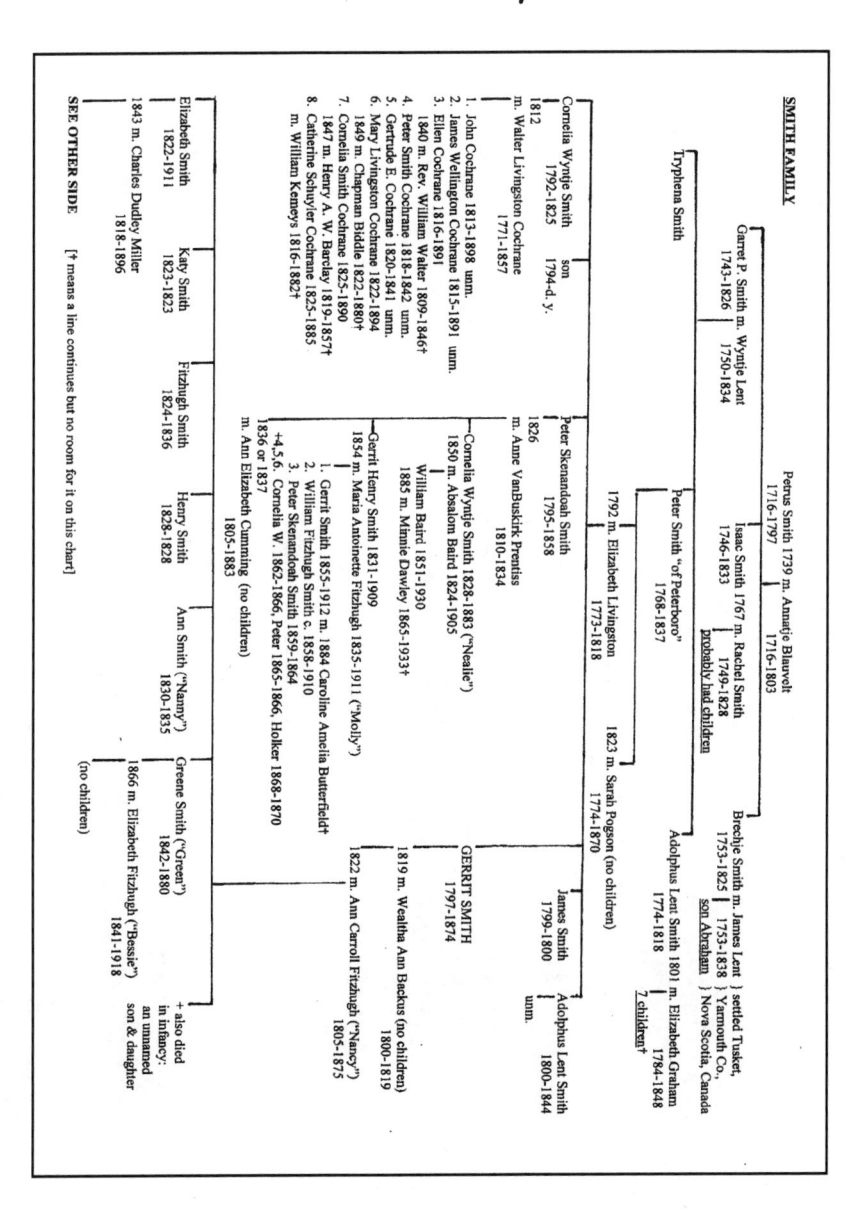

SMITH FAMILY

Petrus Smith 1739 m. Annaetje Blauvelt
1716-1797   1716-1803

- Garret P. Smith m. Wyntje Lent
  1743-1826   1750-1834

- Isaac Smith 1767 m. Rachel Smith } settled Tusket,
  1746-1833   1749-1828   } Yarmouth Co.,
                 probably had children } Nova Scotia, Canada

- Brechje Smith m. James Lent
  1753-1825   1753-1838
  son Abraham

- Adolphus Lent Smith 1801 m. Elizabeth Graham
  1774-1818   1784-1848
                         7 children†

Tryphena Smith

Peter Smith "of Peterboro"
1768-1837

1792 m. Elizabeth Livingston
         1773-1818

1823 m. Sarah Pogson (no children)
         1774-1870

Cornelia Wyntje Smith son 1794-d.y.
1792-1825
1812 m. Walter Livingston Cochrane
         1771-1857

1. John Cochrane 1813-1898 unm.
2. James Wellington Cochrane 1815-1891 unm.
3. Ellen Cochrane 1816-1891
   1840 m. Rev. William Walter 1809-1846†
4. Peter Smith Cochrane 1818-1842 unm.
5. Gertrude E. Cochrane 1820-1841 unm.
6. Mary Livingston Cochrane 1822-1894
   1849 m. Chapman Biddle 1822-1880†
7. Cornelia Smith Cochrane 1825-1890
   1847 m. Henry A. W. Barclay 1819-1857†
8. Catherine Schuyler Cochrane 1825-1885
   m. William Kenays 1816-1821

Peter Skenandoah Smith
1795-1858
1826 m. Anne VanBuskirk Prentiss
         1810-1834

- Cornelia Wyntje Smith 1828-1883 ("Nealie")
  1850 m. Absalom Baird 1824-1905
  - William Baird 1851-1930
    1885 m. Minnie Dawley 1865-1933†
- Gerrit Henry Smith 1831-1909
  1854 m. Maria Antoinette Fitzhugh 1835-1911 ("Molly")
  1. Gerrit Smith 1855-1912 m. 1884 Caroline Amelia Butterfield†
  2. William Fitzhugh Smith c. 1858-1910
  3. Peter Skenandoah Smith 1859-1864
  +4,5,6. Cornelia W. 1862-1866, Peter 1865-1866, Holker 1868-1870
  1836 or 1837
  m. Ann Elizabeth Cumming (no children)
       1805-1883

GERRIT SMITH
1797-1874
1819 m. Wealtha Ann Backus (no children)
         1800-1819
1822 m. Ann Carroll Fitzhugh ("Nancy")
         1805-1875

James Smith   Adolphus Lent Smith
1799-1800   1800-1844
                    unm.

Greene Smith ("Green")
1842-1880
1866 m. Elizabeth Fitzhugh ("Bessie")
         1841-1918
(no children)

Elizabeth Smith   Katy Smith   Fitzhugh Smith   Henry Smith   Ann Smith ("Nanny")
1822-1911   1823-1823   1824-1836   1828-1828   1830-1835
1843 m. Charles Dudley Miller
         1818-1896

SEE OTHER SIDE   [† means a line continues but no room for it on this chart]

+ also died in infancy: an unnamed son & daughter

The Miller Family Tree

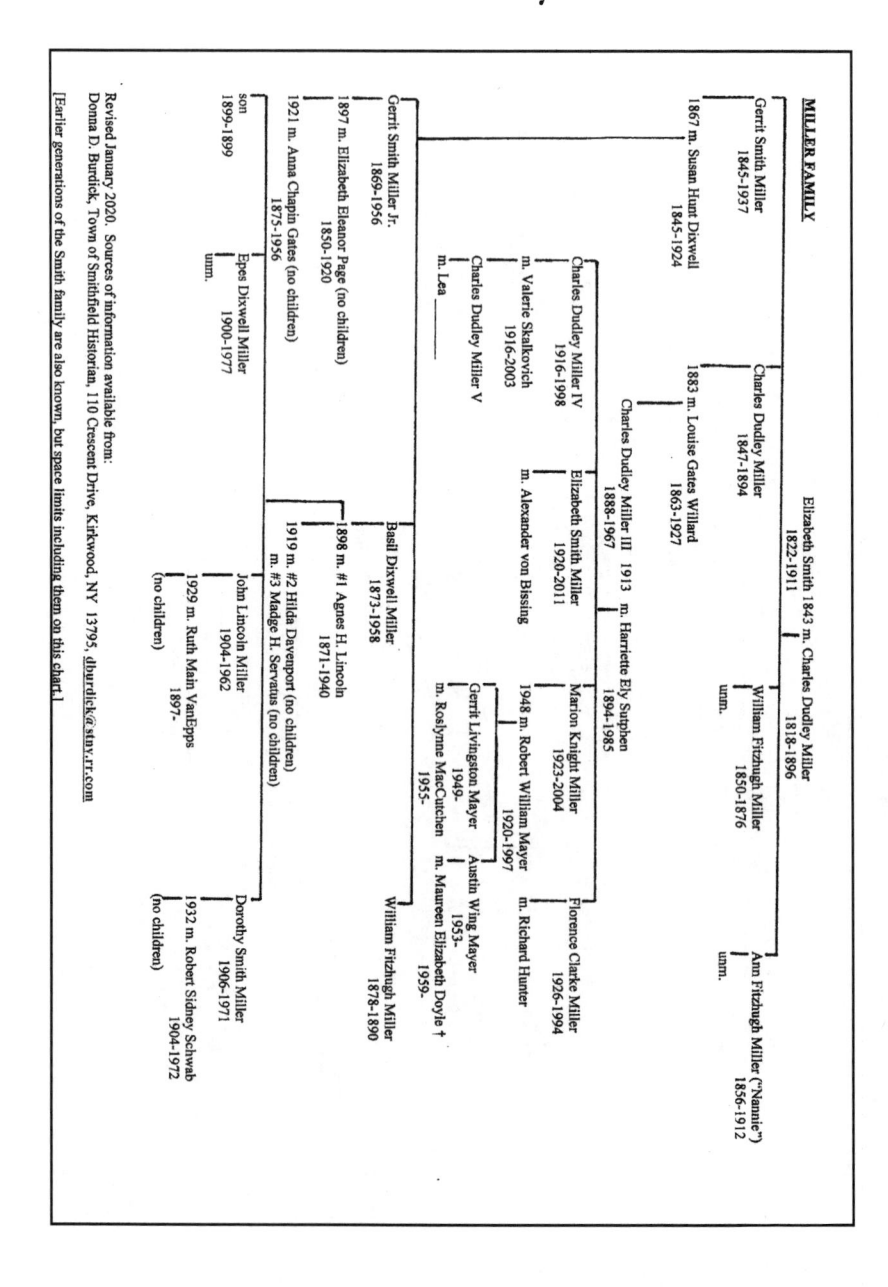

MILLER FAMILY

Elizabeth Smith 1843 m. Charles Dudley Miller
1822-1911   1818-1896

- Gerrit Smith Miller
  1845-1937
  1867 m. Susan Hunt Dixwell
  1845-1924
  - Charles Dudley Miller
    1847-1894
    1883 m. Louise Gates Willard
    1863-1927
    - Charles Dudley Miller III 1913 m. Harriette Ely Sutphen
      1888-1967   1894-1985
      - Charles Dudley Miller IV
        1916-1998
        m. Valerie Skalkovich
        1916-2003
        - Charles Dudley Miller V
          m. Lea _____
      - Elizabeth Smith Miller
        1920-2011
        m. Alexander von Bissing
      - Marion Knight Miller
        1923-2004
        1948 m. Robert William Mayer
        1920-1997
        - Gerrit Livingston Mayer
          1949-
          m. Roslynne MacCutchen
          1955-
        - Austin Wing Mayer
          1953-
          m. Maureen Elizabeth Doyle †
          1959-
      - Florence Clarke Miller
        1926-1994
        m. Richard Hunter
  - Gerrit Smith Miller Jr.
    1869-1956
    1897 m. Elizabeth Eleanor Page (no children)
    1850-1920
    1921 m. Anna Chapin Gates (no children)
    1875-1956
    - son
      1899-1899
    - Epes Dixwell Miller
      1900-1977
      unm.
  - Basil Dixwell Miller
    1873-1958
    1898 m. #1 Agnes H. Lincoln
    1871-1940
    1919 m. #2 Hilda Davenport (no children)
    m. #3 Madge H. Servatus (no children)
    - John Lincoln Miller
      1904-1962
      1929 m. Ruth Main VanEpps
      1897-
      (no children)
    - Dorothy Smith Miller
      1906-1971
      1932 m. Robert Sidney Schwab
      1904-1972
      (no children)

- William Fitzhugh Miller
  1850-1876
  unm.

- Ann Fitzhugh Miller ("Nannie")
  1856-1912
  unm.

William Fitzhugh Miller
1878-1890

Revised January 2020. Sources of information available from:
Donna D. Burdick, Town of Smithfield Historian, 110 Crescent Drive, Kirkwood, NY 13795, dburdick@stny.rr.com

[Earlier generations of the Smith family are also known, but space limits including them on this chart.]

Notes

Abbreviations used in notes

GS — Gerrit Smith
ACS — Ann Carroll Smith
ESM — Elizabeth Smith Miller
CA — George Fitzhugh's book <u>Cannibals All</u>
Soc — George Fitzhugh's book <u>Sociology for the South</u>
SU — Syracuse University Bird Library
MCHS — Madison County Historical Society
PHS — Peterboro Historical Society
HWS — History of Woman Suffrage

Chapter 1—The Pre-reform Era
1. Thomas Herring to Peter Smith, March 20, 1809, SU. For full biographical treatment of Peter Smith, see Dann, Norman K., Peter Smith of Peterboro: Furs, Land and Anguish, Log Cabin Books, 2018.
2. GS to John Thomas, esq., Aug. 27, 1859, SU. For full biographical treatment of Gerrit Smith, see Dann, Norman K., Practical Dreamer: Gerrit Smith and the Crusade for Social Reform, Log Cabin Books, 2009.
3. Stanton, 340-341.
4. Dumond, 151.
5. Cross, 56, 67.
6. Cross, 158.
7. Cross, 81, 28-29.
8. Cross, 101-104.
9. For full biographical treatment of Ann Carroll Fitzhugh Smith, see Dann, Norman K. God, Gerrit, and Guidance: The Life of Ann Carroll Fitzhugh Smith, Log Cabin Books, 2019.
10. For full biographical treatment of Elizabeth Smith Miller, see Dann, Norman K. Ballots, Bloomers, and Marmalade: The Life of Elizabeth Smith Miller, Log Cabin Books, 2016.

Chapter 2—The Reform Era
1. Unity, April 15, 1915; Yellin, 30.
2. Oneida Daily Dispatch, Aug. 26, 1870.
3. The Gerrit Smith Papers, Greene Smith Papers, and Peter Smith Papers are available at Bird Library, Syracuse University.
4. Lewis Tappan to GS, June 15, 1842, SU.
5. GS to John Thomas, Aug. 27, 1859, SU.
6. Frederick Douglass' Paper, May 19, 1854.
7. Frothingham, 143.
8. William F. Fitzhugh to GS, Dec. 5, 1821, SU.
9. ACS to GS, July 18, 1868, SU; Frothingham, 140; Oneida Sachem, April 18, 1858.

10. ACS to ESM, Jan. 17, 1844, SU.
11. Unity, Nov. 19, 1914; New York Tribune, May 16, 1876; Edwin Morton to GrS, Aug. 9, 1875, SU.
12. CS to Bess, Oct. 26, 1873; ACS to ESM, no date, SU.
13. Oneida Telegraph, July 10, 1852.
14. Oneida Democratic Union, Sept. 24, 1930.
15. New York Times, Dec. 29, 1874.
16. Frederick F. Backus to GS, Jan. 22, 1835, SU.
17. Frothingham, 140-141.
18. Unity, Feb. 5, 1914.
19. Galpin.
20. Unity, March 11, 1915.
21. For full biographical treatment of Greene Smith, see Dann, Norman K. Greene Smith and the Wild Life, Log Cabin Books, 2015.

Chapter 3—Abolition
1. GS to Elizabeth Smith, July 16, 1815, SU.
2. GS to John C. Spencer, Nov. 12, 1851, SU.
3. Speech in Peterboro, April 27, 1861, in Sermons and Speeches.
4. George Fitzhugh to GS, Aug. 19, 1850; July 29, 1852; Dec. 25, 1854; April 17, 1851, SU. Elizabeth H. Kelty notebook, 1863-1880, Jan. 31, 1864.
5. Fitzhugh, CA, xvii, 97; Fitzhugh to ACS, March 10, 1855.
6. Fitzhugh, Soc, 189, 256-257.
7. Fitzhugh, Soc, 204; CA, 219.
8. Fitzhugh, CA, xxvii, 237.
9. Fitzhugh to William Lloyd Garrison, Nov. 18, 1856, in CA, 259.
10. Fitzhugh, Soc, 170; CA, 71-78.
11. Fitzhugh, CA, 65; Soc, 206.
12. Fitzhugh, CA, 89-92.
13. Fitzhugh, Soc, 290, 300, 66.
14. Fitzhugh, Soc, 253; Fitzhugh to Professor Holmes, 1855, in CA, xvii. George Fitzhugh to ACS, March 10, 1855.
15. Fitzhugh, Soc, 68-69, 95-96, 85-86.

16. The Liberator, March 6, 13, 1857.
17. Fitzhugh, CA, 8; Soc, 177-179.
18. Fitzhugh, CA, 217-218; Soc, 183, 38.
19. Fitzhugh, Soc, 232-233.
20. Fitzhugh, CA, 228; Soc, 226-227, 258.
21. Fitzhugh to GS, Aug. 14, 1850, SU; Fitzhugh, Soc, 83-84.
22. Fitzhugh, Soc, 251; CA, 199-200.
23. Fitzhugh, CA, 81, 205.
24. Fitzhugh, Soc, 259-271.
25. Fitzhugh, Soc, 248, 250, 277, 287.
26. Fitzhugh, Soc, 43, 61, 245-246; CA, 13, 253-254.
27. Fitzhugh to GS, July 29, 1852; Feb. 25, 1855, SU.
28. Smith/Barnes, 77-78.
29. See John Stauffer, The Black Hearts of Men.
30. GS to John H. Cocke, Dec. 11, 1840, SU.
31. GS speech in Congress, 1854.
32. Hochschild, 93.
33. Speech in Albany, March 13, 1856.
34. GS to John H. Cocke, Dec. 11, 1840, SU.
35. Speech in Congress, May 3, 1854; GS to John C. Spencer, Nov. 12, 1851, SU.
36. Speech in Congress, June 27, 1854; April 6, 1854.
37. For an in-depth treatment of Gerrit Smith's tactics during the abolition movement, see Dann, Norman K. Whatever it Takes, Log Cabin Books, 2011; Kraditor, 168.
38. GS to the editor of the Emancipator, Aug. 23, 1847, MCHS.
39. Unity, Feb. 25, 1915.
40. James G. Birney to GS, Sept. 13, 1835, SU.
41. GS to William Seward, Aug. 11, 1850, SU; For comprehensive treatment of the underground railroad relative to Peterboro and the Smith family, see Dann, Norman K. When We Get to Heaven, Log Cabin Books, 2008.
42. GS to Union Herald editor, Dec. 1, 1838, SU.
43. J.B. Edwards to GS, April 29, 1852, SU.

44. GS to Ezekiel Birdseye, July 8, 1845, SU.
45. GS to the Russell family, Oct. 1, 1841, SU.
46. Dumond, 77.
47. Anti-Slavery Record, 157; 156.
48. W.W. Brown to Wendell Phillips, Nov. 20, 1849 in The Liberator, Nov. 30, 1849.
49. The Liberator, Nov. 30, 1849.
50. Anti-Slavery Record, 172.
51. Weld, 22-24.
52. Rankin, iii-iv.
53. Richmond Daily Dispatch, May 18, 1867.
54. Fitzhugh, CA, xii.

Chapter 4—Women's Rights
1. Wagner, 15; For biographical treatment of Elizabeth Cady Stanton, see Dann, Norman K. Cousins of Reform, Log Cabin Books, 2013.
2. Stanton, The Woman's Bible; Davis, 80.
3. Stanton, Eighty Years, 53, 54.
4. Wagner, 16.
5. Stanton, Eighty Years, 15-16; Verse Book, April 1, 1860, SU.
6. Stanton address to the American Anti-Slavery Society, May 8, 1860; ECS to GS, Dec. 21, 1855, SU.
7. Gordon, 106, 405.
8. Fitzhugh, Soc, 213; CA, 235.
9. Fitzhugh, Soc, 297; GS, Sermons and Speeches, 72-73.
10. Fitzhugh, Soc, 231, 214.
11. Fitzhugh, CA, 131; Soc, 231.
12. Ecker.
13. GS to ECS, Dec. 1, 1855, SU.
14. http://libwww.syr.edu/digital/exhibits/g/GerritSmith/esm.htm
15. Scrapbook 7, 52.
16. Syracuse Daily Courier, June 18, 1857; New York Times, Oct. 15, 1852; Oct. 1, 1851.
17. Faulkner, 72; Wellman, 52.

18. Swerdlow, in Yellin and Van Horne, eds. 32.
19. Albany Register, March 7, 1854.
20. GS to ECS, Dec. 1, 1855, SU.
21. GS to Susan B. Anthony, Dec. 30, 1868, SU; GS to Everett Brown, Aug. 9, 1872, PHS.
22. GS speech in Buffalo, June 14, 1848.
23. Wellman, 217.
24. Colman, 105-106.
25. Frederick Douglass speech at AERA convention, May 12–14, 1869.
26. HWS, II, 923-924.
27. ECS to ESM, Dec. 14, 1867 in Griffith, 128; HWS, III, iv.
28. HWS, II, 333.
29. Faulkner, 207; Griffith, 154; HWS, II, 647, 689, 691, 700; Colman, 154.
30. HWS, II, 714.
31. HWS, IV, 435; Syracuse Journal, June 2, 1911; ESM to GS, Jan. 14, 1869; March 28, 1869, SU.
32. Dann, Ballots..., 151-176.

Chapter 5—Issues Supportive of Reform

1. GS to Chester Dewey, Nov. 9, 1826; GS to Rev. Leonard Bacon, July 23, 1834; ES(M) to Peter Smith, April 25, 1832, SU.
2. Samuel E. Cornish and John B. Russwurm to GS, April 16, 1827, SU.
3. New Haven Journal of Freedom, Aug. 20, 1834; The Liberator, Nov. 8, 1834.
4. GS to Bridge, June 20, 1867.
5. Dann, Practical..., 60–63.
6. GS to John Stuart, Feb. 5, 1869; GS to Greene and Gatty, Dec. 4, 1851, SU.
7. GS to Silas W. Tyler, March 5, 1845; GS to Edwin Heale, June 26, 1841, SU.
8. GS to N. Sanford, Feb. 14, 1840, SU.

9. GS speech, Oct. 9, 1869, SU.
10. Greene to GS, Nov. 26, 1869; Dec. 9, 1869, SU.
11. Verse Book, Oct. 23, 1866, SU.
12. Dann, Ballots..., 77-82.
13. Fletcher Haight to GS, March 22, 1861, SU.
14. Harlow, 67-72.
15. Dann, Practical..., 361-362, 352.
16. Henry Campbell to his sister, June 20, 1851, PHS.

Epilogue
1. Alter, Time, Feb. 3, 2020.

Bibliography

BOOKS

Alter, Charlotte. "Youthquake," <u>Time</u>, Feb. 3, 2020.

Baldwin, James. <u>The Fire Next Time</u>, New York: Dell Publishing, 1964.

Colman, Penny. <u>Elizabeth Cady Stanton and Susan B. Anthony</u>, New York: Henry Holt and Company, 2011.

<u>Correspondence of Gerrit Smith with Albert Barnes</u>, 1868, New York: American News Company.

Cross, Whitney R. <u>The Burned-Over District</u>, Ithaca: Cornell University Press, 1950.

Davis, Sue. <u>The Political Thought of Elizabeth Cady Stanton</u>, New York: New York University Press, 2008.

Dumond, Dwight Lowell. <u>Antislavery: The Crusade for Freedom in America</u>, New York: W.W. Norton, 1961.

Ecker, Sydney W. "Brain Gender Identity," 2009 at aebrain.blogspot.com/2009/05/brain-gender-identity-presentation-by.html

Faulkner, Carol. <u>Lucretia Mott's Heresy: Abolition and Women's Rights in Nineteenth Century America</u>, Philadelphia: University of Pennsylvania, 2011.

Frothingham, Octavius Brooks. <u>Gerrit Smith</u>, 1st ed., New York: G.P. Putnam + Sons, 1878.

Galpin, W.F. <u>Souvenir Program</u>, Aug. 17, 1929.

Gordon, Ann, et. al. <u>The Selected Papers of Elizabeth Cady Stanton and Susan B. Anthony</u>, vol. 1, New Brunswick: Rutgers University Press, 1997.

Harlow, Ralph V. <u>Gerrit Smith</u>, New York: Henry Holt and Company, 1939.

Hochschild, Adam. <u>Bury the Chains: Prophets and Rebels in the Fight to Free an Empire's Slaves</u>, Boston: Houghton Mifflin, 2005.

Kraditor, Aileen. Means and Ends in American Abolitionism, New York: Vintage Books, 1967.
Plakas, Rosemary. Responsible for digitizing seven scrapbooks of Elizabeth Smith Miller and Anne Fitzhugh Miller, online at Library of Congress.
Rankin, John. Letters on American Slavery, Boston: Isaac Knapp, 1838.
Smith, Gerrit. Sermons and Speeches, New York: Ross + Tousey, 1861.
Stanton, Elizabeth Cady. Eighty Years and More, New York: Schocken Books, 1971. Reprinted from T. Fisher Unwin edition of 1898.
Stanton, Elizabeth Cady. The Woman's Bible, New York: The European Publishing Co., 1895- 1898.
Stauffer, John. The Black Hearts of Men, Cambridge: Harvard University Press, 2002.
Wagner, Sally Roesch. The Untold Story of the Iroquois Influence on Early Feminists, Aberdeen, SD: Sky Carrier Press, 1996.
Weld, Theodore Dwight. American Slavery as it Is, New York: The American Anti-Slavery Society, 1839.
Wellman, Judith. The Road to Seneca Falls: Elizabeth Cady Stanton and the First Women's Rights Convention, Chicago: University of Illinois Press, 2004.
Yellin, Jean Fagan and John C. Van Horne, eds. The Abolitionist Sisterhood, Ithaca: Cornell University Press, 1994.
Yellin, Jean Fagan, ed. Incidents in the Life of a Slave Girl, Cambridge: Harvard University Press, 1987.

PERIODICALS

Albany Register, March 7, 1854.
Anti-Slavery Record, vol. III, New York: American Anti-Slavery Society, 1837.
Frederick Douglass' Paper, May 19, 1854.
New Haven Journal of Freedom, Aug. 20, 1834.
New York Times, Oct. 15, 1852; Oct. 1, 1851.

New York Tribune, May 16, 1876.
Oneida Daily Dispatch, Aug. 26, 1870.
Oneida Democratic Union, Sept. 24, 1930.
Oneida Sachem, April 18, 1858.
Oneida Telegraph, July 10, 1852.
Richmond Daily Dispatch, May 18, 1867.
Syracuse Daily Courier, June 18, 1857.
Syracuse Journal, June 2, 1911.
The Liberator, Nov. 30, 1849.
Unity, April 15, 1915; Nov. 19, 1914.

WEBSITES

www.syr.edu/digital/exhibits/g/GerritSmith/esm.htm
www.tolerance.org/hardhistory

Index

13th Amendment 61
14th Amendment 61, 139
15th Amendment 61, 139
16th Amendment 140
100-Acre tract, the 25,
3/5 rule 15,
abolition movement, the ix, 22, 23, 29, 32, 80, 81, 110-113, 116, 149
Adby, Edward Strutt 114
Africa 80, 150
African-Americans 15, 67, 80, 161
African-American rights 119
Albany, NY 20
Albany Register 134
alcoholism 41,
Alter, Charlotte 164
American Anti-Slavery Society 104, 133, 150
American Colonization Society 80, 100, 149, 150
American Equal Rights Association 139
American Peace Society 111
American Woman Suffrage Association 139
"American Slavery as it Is" 116
Anderson, Thomas 72
Anthony, Susan B. viii, 61, 136, 140
Astor, John Jacob 13,
Audubon, John James 64
Backus, Frederick 26, 58,
Backus, Wealtha 26,

Baird, Spencer F. 64
Baldwin, James 166
Baptists 43,
Beardsley, Charles 81
Bell, John Graham 64
Belleville, NJ 64
Berea College 151
Bible, the 120
Binghamton, NY 20,
Birdhouse, the 64, 65, 142
Birney, James Gillespie 16, 61, 81, 84, 103, 104
Blackman, Harriet and Maurice 72
Black History Month 119
Black Lives Matter 165
black people 13,
bloomers 130, 131
Boston, MA 18, 19, 82, 100, 111, 138, 155
Boyle, James 22,
Brigham Young University Archives 120
Briton 16,
Brown, George 59,
Brown, John 40, 55, 61, 96, 111, 112, 116, 163
Brown, Mary 72
Brown, William Wells 114
Brownson, Orestes 22,
Buchanan, President James 83
Buffalo, NY 20,
Burchard, Jedediah 22,

Bunker Hill 16,
Calvinism 19,
Campbell, John and Martha 72
Campbell, Henry 157
Canada 59, 107, 108
Canandaigua, NY 141
Carroll, Charles 48
Carroll, John 25
Carroll, Rebecca 26
Central New York 20-22, 143
Chase, Samuel P. 61
Chewsville, MD 25
Chicago, IL 141
Chile 164
Christianity 24-26, 44, 80, 86, 103-104, 112, 119, 150
Churchill, Winston 161
Civil Rights Movement 166
Civil War, the 61, 94, 96, 117, 137, 157
Civil War Weekend 163
Clifton Springs, NY 143
Clinton, NY 77, 151
Cochrane, Cornelia Smith 51
Colfax, Schuyler 154
Communism 92
Connecticut 21, 113
conservative politics 22
Cook, Elder 59
Cornell, Ezra 42
Cornell University 42
Corning, NY 59
Corning, William 59
Cornish, Samuel Eli 150
Coues, Elliot 64
Cross, Whitney 21

cruelty toward slaves 105-107
Dartmouth College 151
Darwin, Charles 67
Davis, Jefferson 117
Davis, Mildred 72
Declaration of Independence 77, 89, 97
Declaration of Sentiments 137
DeGroat, Carl and Ximena 72
Democratic Party 23, 43, 99, 102
Dorrance, Donna 72
Dorrance, James and Maude 72
Dorrance, Mary 72
Douglass, Frederick 31, 55, 61, 81, 82, 96, 116, 138, 139
Douglas, Aaron 59
Douglas, William Henry 59
dress reform 78, 129, 141
Dwight, Timothy 113
Edinburgh Review 114
Edwards, John B. 107, 108
egalitarianism 20
Elizabeth Smith Miller Study Club 146
Elizabeth Smith Miller Tea 163
Ellis, Seymour and Sylvia 72
Emancipation Day 163
Emancipation Proclamation 166
Emerson, Ralph Waldo 18, 19
environmental issues 163
Erie Canal, the 20
evangelism 22, 23
Euro-Christian culture 127
Evans Academy viii, 73, 150, 151
Federalism 19
Field Ornithology 64
Finney, Charles Grandison 21, 22
Fitzhugh, George 82-93, 96, 117, 125, 126

Index

Fitzhugh, James 108
Fitzhugh, William Frisby 25, 47, 48, 55, 108
Flores, Joe 138
Foster, Abby Kelley 123, 132, 133
Frank, Carl 72
Franklin, Benjamin 81
Free Church movement 24, 34, 103
Free Church of Peterboro viii, 43, 44, 104
Framingham, MA 15
Frost, Robert 164
Frothingham, Octavius Brooks 42
Fuller, James C. 109
Garrison, William Lloyd viii, 15, 55, 61, 81, 82, 88, 100, 150
gay rights 119
gender issues 41, 127
Geneva, NY 142
Geneva Historical Society 143
Geneva Political Equality Club 143, 146
Gerrit Smith Birthday Celebration 163
Gerrit Smith estate 11, 37, 47, 52, 53-55, 57, 163
Gerrit Smith Estate National Historic Landmark 164
Gerrit Smith papers 48
God 19,
Golden Rule, the viii, 18, 36, 97, 159
Gonzalez, Emma 165
Grant, Ulysses 141
Gray, John P. 112
Greeley, Horace 61
Green, Beriah 63, 81, 121, 150, 151
Green New Deal, the 165
Greene Smith papers 48
Grimké, Angelina 17, 64, 116, 123, 128, 132
Grimké, Sarah 17
Grove, the 57
Hagerstown, MD 25, 47, 59
Haight, Fletcher N. 155
Haines, William 59
Haiti 59
Hall, Doris 72
Hameister, Jade 165
Hamilton College 41, 78, 94, 151
Hampton Agricultural Institute 151
Harpers Ferry, WV 111
Harvard University 56, 57
Henry, Patrick 14
Hermaphrodism 127
"History of Woman Suffrage" 77
Hive, the 25
Holley, Myron 103
Hong Kong 164
Howard University 151
Huller, Donald and Joan 72
human rights vii, ix, 13, 27, 129
Hunt, Judge Ward 141
Huntley, Prof. Taze and Ginnia 72
India 164
interracial education 44
In The Kitchen 154
Iran 164
Iraq 164
Jacksonian democracy 19, 22
Jackson, James Caleb 33
Jacobs, Harriet 34
Jefferson, Thomas 14, 115 160

Index

Jim Crow laws 62
Johnson, Boris 162
Johnson, Charles 59
Johnson, Peter 59
Judd, Leon 72
Kansas 140
Keeney, Elisha 140
Kentucky 108, 149
King, Caroline 60
Kraditor, Aileen 101
Ladies Domestic Seminary 151
Langberg, Bessie 72
Lebanon 164
Lexington, CT 16
LGBTQ+ issues 166
Liberty League Convention 137
liberal thought 20
Liberty Party, the 24, 43, 102, 116
Lincoln, Abraham 103, 166
Livingston family 121
Lochland estate 142, 143, 146
Lovejoy, Elijah 81 100
Lutheran General Assembly 115
Lutheran Synod of Illinois 115
Madison County Children's Home of Peterboro viii, 161, 162
Madison County Historical Society 14
Madison, James 160
Marjory Stoneman Douglas High School 165
Maryland 25, 48, 108
Maryland Historical Trust 25
matriarchal society 121
McElligott, Tommy 60
Mercer, Charles Fenton 100
Methodists 43
Miller, Anne Fitzhugh 142, 143
Miller, Charles Dudley 55, 129, 142, 155
Miller, Elizabeth Smith vii, 26, 35, 48, 55, 57, 60, 123, 128-131, 141-146, 149, 150, 154
Miller, Jack 72
Millerites 34
Milwaukee, WI 137
Mississippi 108, 109
moral reformers 60-62
moral suasion 81, 101
Morrisville, NY 152
Morton, Edwin 56
Mott, Lucretia 131-133, 136
Munderback, Minnie 72
Nash, Duplissis 156
National Abolition Hall of Fame & Museum, 12, 73, 74, 138, 163
National Register of Historic Places 73
National Woman Suffrage Association 139, 141
native Americans 13, 121
Natural Law 97, 122, 137
natural selection 67
New England Puritans 126
New Englanders 31
New Haven, CT 85
New Jersey 21
New York Central College 151
New York City 46
New York City harbor 147
<u>New York Commercial Advertiser</u> 132
New York state 12, 147
New York State Anti-Slavery Society 74, 81
New York State Constitution 146

Index

New York State Judicial Committee 146
New York State Legislature 134
New York State Woman Suffrage Association 146
New York Times, the 58, 131
New York Tribune, the 61
North Carolina 60
Oberlin College 151
Ohio 17
Ohio River 17
Oneida Institute 151
Oneida Nation 121, 122, 127
"On the Origin of Species" 67
Oswego Canal 107
Oswego, NY 20, 107, 108, 151, 156
Packwood, Downer and Marjorie 72
Parkland, FL 165
Paterson, NJ 59
Perfectionism 17
Peterboro Area Historical Society 71
Peterboro businesses 52
Peterboro, NY vii, viii, ix, x, 12, 32, 42, 45, 47, 52, 53, 59-62, 67, 82, 93, 107, 108, 121, 142, 149, 163
Peterboro Old Home Day 71
Peterboro Presbyterian Church 73, 74
Peterboro Temperance Hotel 155, 161
Peter, Paul & Mary 166
Peter Smith papers 48
Phelps, NY 143
Philadelphia Register, the 46
philanthropy 41-43, 53, 159-163
Phillips, Wendell 55, 85, 114, 138
Political Equality Study Class 146

Port Byron 59
Pre-Reform Era, the 14, 26, 27, 29
Presbyterians 43
Puritanism 19
Quakers, the 21
Ramsey, James 98
Rankin, John 17, 116
Reformed Drunkards' Society of the Town of Smithfield 157
Reform Era, the vii, ix, 27
Religion of Reason, the 112
Republican party, the 23, 43, 103
Richland, VA 117
Rochester, Nathaniel 25, 48
Rochester, NY 20, 25, 48, 140
Rockland County, NY 13
Rowe, the Rev. Robert 71
Royal Port Virginia 83
Russell, Malvina 109, 110
Russell, Samuel 108
Russwurm, John Brown 150
Salem witch hunt, the 126
Sanborn, Franklin Benjamin 56, 111
Schuyler family 121
Sebring, Jan and John 72
Second Coming of Christ, the 17
Second Great Awakening, the 16, 19, 23, 24
Secret Six, the 56
Seneca Falls, NY 136, 137
Seneca Falls Convention 137, 138
Seneca Lake 142
Seward, William 105
sexual orientation 127
Shakers, the 21, 34
Sims, Harriet 108, 110
sin 18

Index

slave owners 14, 47
slavery (the institution) 15, 23, 31, 97, 113, 160
Smith, Ann Carroll Fitzhugh vii, vii, 13, 24-26, 35, 38, 39, 47, 49-51, 53, 57, 61, 62, 110, 112, 121, 126, 132, 139, 159
Smith, Elizabeth Livingston 41, 55
Smith family, the ix, 36, 40, 77, 80, 101, 112, 126, 159, 162, 167
Smith, Bessie 57
Smith, Gerrit vii, vii, ix, 13, 15, 19, 24, 31-36, 38, 39, 42, 44-51, 53, 59-62, 77, 93-112, 121-126, 128, 135, 136, 138-140, 150-153, 159, 166-167
Smith, Greene vii, 35, 56, 57, 63-67, 112, 142, 153, 154
Smith Land Office, the 163
Smith, Mollie and Myron 72
Smith, Peter 13, 14, 35, 41, 46, 47, 55, 80, 150
Smithfield Community Association 73
Social Security 164
Spencer, Herbert 119
Stanton, Elizabeth Cady vii, ix, 19, 31, 32, 40, 61, 77, 96, 119-128, 133-136, 139-141
Stanton, Henry B. 96, 121, 122, 134
Statue of Liberty 147
Stewart, Margaret 72
Stoker, Margaret 72
Stuart, Alvan 103
Sumner, Charles 40, 55, 61
SUNY Morrisville 72
Syracuse, NY 20
Syracuse Daily Courier 131

Tappan, Lewis 43
Tappan, NY 64
taxidermy 64
temperance 79, 80, 135, 153-157
Tennessee 17
testosterone 128
The American Society for the Promotion of Temperance 155
The Liberator newspaper 88, 100
The London Evangelical Magazine 114
The New Haven Journal of Freedom 150
The Revolution 141
Thomas, George 60
Thoreau, Henry David 18
Time magazine 164
Town of Smithfield 157
Transcendentalism 17, 18
Treaty of Ghent, the 20
Trump, Donald J. 163
Truth, Sojourner 163
Tubman, Harriet 116, 163
Tucker, Mildred and Walter Sr. 72
Typhoid fever 112
Underground Railroad 104, 107
Union Herald newspaper 105
Upstate New York 102, 108
U.S. Congress 46, 97, 139, 157, 165
U.S. Constitution, the 15, 61-62, 77, 138
U.S. Dept. of the Interior 73, 163
U.S. Senate 140
Utica, NY 20, 41, 81
Utica Asylum for the Insane 112
Van Rensselaer family 121
Virginia 14, 84, 98
Wagner, Sally Roesch 122

Walker, Dr. Mary 131
War of 1812, the 20
Washington, D.C. 83
Washington, George 14, 41, 81
Weld, Theodore Dwight 64, 82, 115
Whig Party, the 24, 99, 102
white male supremacy viii
William Smith College for Women 146
Williams, Arthur and Olive 72
Williams, James and Ellen 72
Wilson, Hiram 63
Whittier, John Greenleaf 61, 82
woman suffrage 62, 78, 124, 136, 140, 141

Woman Suffrage Convention in Geneva, NY 143-146
Women's Anti-Slavery Convention 81, 132
Women's History Month 119
women's rights movement, the ix, x, 17, 27, 78, 119-136, 149, 160
Women's Rights Convention 136
World Anti-Slavery Convention 133
World War II 161
Worthington, Samuel 108
Yale University 113

Acknowledgements

A salute of sincere appreciation is due to those
who aided my research efforts:

The staff of Syracuse University George Arents Research Library, Department of Special Collections

The staff of the Madison County Historical Society, Oneida, New York

Town of Smithfield Historian Donna Dorrance Burdick

The constant support of my partner in life, Dorothy Harrington Willsey-Dann

About the Author

This is the ninth book by Norman Kingsford Dann, Ph.D. He was born in Providence, RI in 1940. After graduating from Mt. Pleasant High School, he spent three years in the U.S. Navy as an aviation electronics technician. He earned a bachelor of arts degree in psychology from Alderson-Broaddus College in Philippi, WV and a master of arts in Political Science from the University of Rhode Island. He was graduated from Syracuse University in 1974 with a Ph.D. in Interdisciplinary Social Sciences. In 1999, he retired after 33 years on the faculty of the Social Sciences Department at Morrisville State College.

In retirement, Norm has specialized in research and writing on the abolition movement, with several articles and book reviews in publication. He published his first book, *When We Get to Heaven: Runaway Slaves on the Road to Peterboro*, in 2008. His second book in 2009 was a full biography that capped more than 15 years of research on abolitionist Gerrit Smith. It is titled *Practical Dreamer: Gerrit Smith and the Crusade for Social Reform*. His third book, *Whatever It Takes: The Antislavery Movement and the Tactics of Gerrit Smith*, came out in 2011. His fourth book, *Cousins of Reform: Elizabeth Cady Stanton and Gerrit Smith*, was published in 2013. His fifth book, *Greene Smith and the WildLife: The Story of Peterboro's Avid Outdoorsman*, was published in 2015. His sixth book, *Ballots, Bloomers & Marmalade: The Life of Elizabeth Smith Miller*, premiered in 2016. His seventh book, *Peter Smith of Peterboro: Furs, Land and Anguish*, appeared in 2018. His eighth book, *God, Gerrit & Guidance: The Life of Ann Carroll Fitzhugh Smith*, was published in 2019.

His other interests include sterling silver craft work. He creates jewelry pieces and specializes in silver plaques, including a centerpiece of Madison County's bicentennial celebration in 2006. Norm also enjoys archery hunting for whitetail deer and maintains a large vegetable garden. He cultivates hop plants for display and sale through the annual Madison County Hop Fest.

Norm has dedicated his retirement to sharing the story of local history regarding abolition and the Gerrit Smith family. He is a member of the Peterboro-based Smithfield Community Association and the Peterboro Historical Society, and is a founding member of the National Abolition Hall of Fame & Museum.

Other Books by Norman K. Dann

When We Get to Heaven:
Runaway Slaves on the Road to Peterboro
(2008)

Practical Dreamer:
Gerrit Smith and the Crusade for Social Reform
(2009)

Whatever It Takes:
The Antislavery Movement
and the Tactics of Gerrit Smith
(2011)

Cousins of Reform:
Elizabeth Cady Stanton and Gerrit Smith
(2013)

Greene Smith and the WildLife:
The Story of Peterboro's Avid Outdoorsman
(2015)

Ballots, Bloomers & Marmalade:
The Life of Elizabeth Smith Miller
(2016)

Peter Smith of Peterboro:
Furs, Land and Anguish
(2018)

God, Gerrit & Guidance
The Life of Ann Carroll Fitzhugh Smith
(2019)

All titles from
Log Cabin Books of Hamilton, NY.
www.logcabinbooks.com